HARRY S.
TRUMAN

HARRY S. TRUMAN

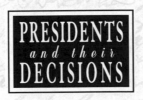

HARRY S. TRUMAN

LAURA K. EGENDORF, *Book Editor*

BONNIE SZUMSKI, *Editorial Director*
SCOTT BARBOUR, *Managing Editor*
JAMES D. TORR, *Series Editor*

GREENHAVEN PRESS, INC.
SAN DIEGO, CALIFORNIA

Every effort has been made to trace the owners of copyrighted material. The articles in this volume may have been edited for content, length, and/or reading level. The titles have been changed to enhance the editorial purpose.

Library of Congress Cataloging-in-Publication Data

Harry S. Truman / Laura Egendorf, book editor.
     p. cm. — (Presidents and their decisions)
     Includes bibliographical references (p.) and index.
     ISBN 0-7377-0919-7 (lib. bdg. : alk. paper) — ISBN 0-7377-0918-9 (pbk. : alk. paper)
     1. Truman, Harry S., 1884–1972. 2. United States—Foreign relations—1945–1953—Decision making. 4. United States—Military policy—Decision making. I. Egendorf, Laura K., 1973–   II. Series.

E813 .H368 2002
973.918'092—dc21
                                                                    2001033510
                                                                    CIP

Cover photo: © Bettmann/CORBIS
ACME News Pictures–UPI, 45
Library of Congress, 174
Smithsonian Institution, 91
U.S. Army, courtesy of the Harry S. Truman Library, 18

Series Design: LiMiTeD Edition Book Design, Linda Mae Tratechaud

© 2002 Greenhaven Press, Inc.
P.O. Box 289009, San Diego, CA 92198-9009

PRINTED IN THE U.S.A.

Contents

Chapter 1: Dropping the Atomic Bomb on Japan

CHAPTER 2: THE TRUMAN DOCTRINE AND THE REBUILDING OF EUROPE

on President Truman's part. Truman was guided by his
desire to avoid war with the Soviet Union.

CHAPTER 3: THE KOREAN WAR

Chapter 4: Truman's Domestic Policies

FOREWORD

“THE PRESIDENCY OF THE UNITED STATES IS OFTEN DE-scribed as the most powerful office in the world,” writes Forrest McDonald in *The American Presidency: An Intellectual History*. “In one sense this description is accurate,” he says, “for even casual decisions made in the White House can affect the lives of millions of people.” But McDonald also notes that presidential power “is restrained by the countervailing power of Congress, the courts, the bureaucracy, popular opinion, the news media, and state and local governments. What presidents do have is awesome responsibilities combined with unique opportunities to persuade others to do their bidding—opportunities enhanced by the possibility of dispensing favors, by the mystique of presidential power, and by the aura of monarchy that surrounds the president.”

The way various presidents have used the complex power of their office is the subject of Greenhaven Press's Presidents and Their Decisions series. Each volume in the series examines one particular president and the key decisions he made while in office.

Some presidential decisions have been made in a relatively brief period of time, as with Abraham Lincoln's suspension of the writ of habeus corpus at the start of the Civil War. Others were refined as they were implemented over a period of years, as was the case with Franklin Delano Roosevelt's struggle to lead the country out of the Great Depression. Some presidential actions are generally lauded by historians—for example, Lyndon Johnson's support of the civil rights movement in the 1960s—while others have been condemned—such as Richard Nixon's efforts, from 1972 to 1974, to cover up the involvement of his aides in the Watergate scandal.

Most of the truly history-making presidential decisions, though, remain the subject of intense scrutiny and historical debate. Many of these were made during a time of war or other crisis, in which a president was forced to risk either spectacular success or devastating failure. Examples include Lincoln's much-scrutinized handling of the crisis at Fort Sumter, the first conflict of the Civil War; FDR's efforts to aid the European Allies at the beginning of World War II; Harry Truman's controversial decision to use the atomic bomb in order to end that conflict; and Lyndon Johnson's fateful decision to escalate the war in Vietnam.

Each volume in the Presidents and Their Decisions series devotes a full chapter to each of the president's key decisions. The essays in each chapter, most written by presidential historians and biographers, offer a range of perspectives on the president and his actions. Some provide background on the political, social, and economic factors behind a particular decision. Others critique the president's performance, offering a negative or positive appraisal. Essays have been chosen for their concise and engaging presentation of the facts, and each is preceded by a straightforward summary of the article's content.

In addition to the articles, these books include extensive material to help the student researcher. An opening essay provides both a brief biography of the president and an overview of the events that occurred during his time in office. A chronology also helps readers keep track of the dates of specific events. A comprehensive index and an annotated table of contents aid readers in quickly locating material of interest, and an extensive bibliography serves as a launching point for further research. Finally, an appendix of primary historical documents provides a sampling of the president's most important speeches, as well as some of his contemporaries' criticisms.

Greenhaven Press's Presidents and Their Decisions series will help students gain a deeper understanding of the decisions made by some of the most influential leaders in American history.

Harry S. Truman: A Biography

A LL U.S. VICE PRESIDENTS FACE THE PROSPECT OF BECOM-
ing president, if the president they serve under were
to die. However, only a handful of vice presidents have
found themselves in that position, and fewer still have in-
herited responsibilities similar to those that Harry S. Truman did on April 12, 1945, the day that Franklin Delano
Roosevelt died. Not only did Truman become president on
that day, he succeeded the man who had been president for
an unprecedented twelve years, the man who had led the
United States through the Great Depression and almost to
the end of the Second World War. Truman—who had been
vice president for less than three months—would be responsible for ensuring America's victory over the Axis powers of Germany, Italy, and Japan. Four months after he was
sworn in, Truman would become the postwar president.

The decisions Truman made during his eight years in
office helped shape the postwar society that established
America as both the most powerful democratic nation in
the world and the principal opposition to the twin communist threats of the Soviet Union and China. Under Truman's leadership, the United States entered the Cold War, a
rivalry that would dominate world politics for the next
forty-five years.

Truman's Childhood and Youth

Harry S. Truman, born on May 8, 1884, in Lamar, Mis-
souri, was the eldest child of John Anderson Truman and
Martha Ellen Truman. "Harry" was in honor of his uncle
Harrison Young. The "S." had no specific meaning, though
it likely was an homage to both grandfathers, Solomon
Young and Anderson Shipp Truman.

For the first six years of Harry's life, the Trumans lived on various Missouri farms. In 1890, the family moved to Independence, Missouri. That year, in Sunday school, Truman noticed a pretty five-year-old girl named Elizabeth Virginia Wallace—known to her friends and family as Bess. The Trumans remained in Independence until 1902, with Harry graduating from high school in 1901. Then the family moved to Kansas City, Missouri, after John Truman lost $40,000 in grain speculation.

Unable to afford college, Harry and his brother Vivian worked as bank clerks. They held jobs at various banks until 1906, when the Trumans—who also had a daughter, Mary Jane—moved to the farm in Grandview, Missouri, that was owned by Martha's mother. Harry helped run the farm until 1917. According to Truman biographer Robert H. Ferrell, the years spent on the farm were important to Harry's development:

> Truman's preparation for the presidency began with his early life on the farm, the kind of experience that many a lad in the years before and just after the turn of the twentieth century never forgot. . . . After 1950 it no longer was important for politicians to boast that they had been born and raised on a farm. For Truman, however, the farm was the essential beginning.[1]

A Soldier and a Husband

For thirty-three years, Harry Truman's life had not extended beyond Missouri. In April 1917, that changed. In 1914, the Great War had begun in Europe. The United States had not participated in the first years of the conflict, except for leading negotiations in an effort to end the war. However, after Germany's January 1917 announcement that it would begin unrestricted submarine warfare against shipping to and from Britain, the United States broke diplomatic relations with Germany and declared war on April 6. President Wilson called up the National Guard, which Harry had joined in 1905. Although Harry was the sole financial support for his mother and sister (his father having died in 1914) and was two years older than the upper age limit set by the Selective Service Act, he chose to rejoin the National Guard and take his part in the war. Lieutenant Truman reported for duty in Oklahoma soon after Wilson's announcement and was sent to France in March 1918; he was promoted to captain the next month.

Truman became the commander of Battery D of the 2nd Battalion, 129th Field Artillery—or, as they were nicknamed, "Dizzy D." He led his troops in the Meuse-Argonne offensive of September–October 1918 and then to Verdun in the final month of the war. No one in Battery D died under Truman's command; the one fatality occurred on a special detail. Truman and the rest of the 129th Field Artillery sailed back to America in April 1919. Truman's leadership skills were evident in the war; he was able to win his troops' respect without berating or humiliating them. According to one soldier, as cited in David McCullough's biography of Truman: "'He had, as an older man, a very quiet sort of way of serving as a leader. . . . And he was a disciplinarian but he was very fair."[2]

Now that Harry was safely back from Europe, he could at last wed Bess Wallace. Harry had courted her for years through letters and visits, and they became engaged before he left for the war. The couple wed on June 28, 1919, and moved into her mother's home.

Following the war, Harry and Eddie Jacobson—whom Harry had befriended in Oklahoma—opened a men's clothing store in Kansas City. The store was successful in its first year, but the American economy began to struggle in the early 1920s and Truman & Jacobson closed in 1922, its owners $35,000 in debt. Truman had failed as a businessman, but he would soon find success in politics.

The Pendergast Machine

In 1920s Missouri, the most powerful force in Democratic politics was the Pendergast family. Jim Pendergast was a Kansas City alderman who for eighteen years reached out to his fellow Irish and to various immigrant groups. Mc-Cullough writes: "The peak of his power came after the turn of the century. . . . By then he had picked his own mayor, James A. ('Fighting Jim') Reed, in addition to every other key office at City Hall."[3] When Jim died in 1911, his brother Tom took on the mantle. Tom Pendergast was tremendously popular in Kansas City, where he provided thousands of jobs. McCullough notes that the people to whom Pendergast gave jobs often repaid him by voting "early and often" on election days.[4]

Truman was friends with Tom Pendergast's nephew, Jim. A few months before Truman & Jacobson closed, Jim and his father Mike—another leader of the Pendergast machine—asked Truman if he wanted to run for the eastern judge of Jackson County. Truman accepted and won the election. He was sworn in on January 1, 1923. Truman would fail in a reelection bid two years later, but that would be the only election he would ever lose. In November 1926, with the support of the Pendergasts, he won election as a presiding judge. He would remain in politics for the next twenty-seven years. By 1926, Truman was also a father; Bess had given birth to Mary Margaret Truman on February 17, 1924.

Truman served two four-year terms as a presiding judge. He was in charge of an annual budget of $7 million, two courthouses, 700 employees (including sheriff, superintendent of schools, and county treasurer), the county hospital, the county's home for the aged, and three homes for neglected children and young criminals. One of his most significant accomplishments was the creation of a modern road system for Jackson County.

In 1934, Tom Pendergast asked Truman if he was interested in running for the U.S. Senate. Truman agreed and defeated John Cochran that November. In his biography, *Truman: The Rise to Power*, Richard Lawrence Miller suggests that Truman benefited from the Pendergast machinery in that election. "The Pendergast machine was in grand form when election day arrived. . . . At one polling place [Truman] watched men going round and round in a circle, casting one ballot after another. Situation normal."[5]

Harry S. Truman

Many people questioned Truman's ties with the Pendergasts, because of the considerable, and possibly illegal, power that the family held. The Pendergast machine lost its power in 1939 after Tom Pendergast was convicted of income tax evasion. He served one year at Leavenworth Prison. In her biography of her father, Margaret Truman criticizes those who suggested Harry was unduly influenced by the Pendergast machine. According to Margaret, "[My father] had already made it clear that he had the backing and ability to run a pretty good race on his own. Thus there never was and never would be any subservience in his relationship with the Pendergasts. But there was another element, which some of Dad's critics have mistaken for subservience—party loyalty."[6]

While Pendergast might have helped Truman win the election, the connection tainted his early years as a senator. Many of his cohorts looked down on Truman because of the Pendergast connection. Overall, Truman did not accomplish much during his first term as senator, other than his part in the writing of 1938's Civil Aeronautics Act and the Transportation Act of 1940, also known as the Wheeler-

Truman Bill, named for Truman and Senator Burton Wheeler of Montana. The junior senator from Missouri also found himself in conflict with President Roosevelt, partly because Truman was a stronger supporter of labor unions. Although Truman consistently voted for New Deal programs, he found himself ignored by Roosevelt in favor of Missouri's senior senator, Bennett Clark.

1940–1944: Truman Gains Prominence

Truman won reelection to the Senate in 1940. By that time, World War II had been raging for over a year. A few days into Truman's second term, Roosevelt announced his Lend-Lease program, which would provide Great Britain with weapons.

World War II helped Truman gain attention on the national political scene. After hearing complaints about profiteering at Army camps, he visited a variety of camps throughout the United States and became aware of the shabby and incomplete construction that was prevalent. Concerned about what he saw, Truman proposed that a committee be formed to study the awarding of defense contracts. The Senate Special Committee to Investigate the National Defense Program was approved in March 1941. Known better as the Truman Committee, the senators inspected nine camps, discovering cost overruns and inefficiency. They also investigated the American munitions industry, discovering poor workmanship and shortages in aluminum, copper, rubber, and zinc. The committee would eventually issue fifty reports and hold more than 400 hearings. In the end, the Truman Committee not only saved the country a huge sum of money—possibly as much as $15 billion—but also led to the production of higher-quality military equipment.

The hearings held by the Truman Committee revealed an important aspect of its chairman's character. McCullough writes: "When presiding, he seemed invariably well prepared and in charge, yet he seldom dominated. . . . No one could remember congressional hearings being handled with such straightforwardness and intelligence."[7]

Thrust into the Presidency

Speculation that Roosevelt would name Truman his vice president, if the president were to run for a fourth term, began in 1943. Although Truman said in 1944 that he was not seeking the nomination, he was nominated that summer in Chicago. Truman remained reluctant but was convinced after having a telephone conversation with Roosevelt. The Roosevelt-Truman ticket triumphed over Thomas E. Dewey and John W. Bricker in the general election.

Truman had one of America's shortest tenures as vice president, serving less than three months. Roosevelt's health had long been failing, and he died in Warm Springs, Georgia, on April 12, 1945. It was now Truman's responsibility to bring World War II to a conclusion.

The European portion of the war was decided soon after Truman's swearing-in. Italy had already surrendered to the Allies. On April 20, the U.S. Seventh Army captured the German city of Nürnberg, while on April 24, the Soviet army ringed Berlin. Adolf Hitler killed himself in a Berlin bunker on April 30. One week later, at General Dwight Eisenhower's headquarters, German general Alfred Jodl signed an unconditional surrender.

The Decision to Drop the Bomb

The Allied forces were victorious in Europe, but the fighting in the Pacific continued. The Allies sought unconditional surrender from Japan, but the Japanese military was still fighting intensely and had given few signs that they would soon give up. The Battle of Okinawa, which began on April 1 and lasted until June 21, was one of the deadliest campaigns of the war, leading to the deaths of more than 100,000 Japanese soldiers and an additional 48,000 American casualties.

In order to defeat Japan, it appeared a new weapon would have to be used. The development of that weapon—the atomic bomb—had begun in 1939, when the process of fission was discovered. The Manhattan Project began in 1942. Led by physicist J. Robert Oppenheimer at the laboratories in Los Alamos, New Mexico, it was an effort to design and build the first atomic bombs.

On May 9, 1945, a group of nine men known as the Interim Committee met to discuss plans for the atomic bomb. Truman did not attend the meetings, instead sending his adviser Jimmy Byrnes as a personal representative. After holding several sessions, the committee concluded the bomb should be dropped on Japanese war plants and used without warning. The atomic bomb was tested on July 21 in Los Alamos, New Mexico, and declared a success. Truman was in Potsdam, Germany, at the time, in a conference with Soviet leader Joseph Stalin and British prime minister Winston Churchill.

Truman approved the bombing of Japan on July 25. The next day, the United States, Great Britain, and China issued a declaration asking Japan to unconditionally surrender; Japan refused. The first bomb was dropped on Hiroshima the morning of August 6, killing 75,000 people instantly and more than 50,000 in the ensuing months from the effects of radiation. Japan still would not surrender, so Truman allowed a second bomb to fall on Nagasaki; that bomb left another 75,000 Japanese dead or wounded. Finally, on August 14, 1945, Japan surrendered, with the assurances that the Japanese emperor could remain. After almost six years, World War II was over.

The bombing of Japan was Truman's first major—and possibly his most controversial—decision. In the more than half-century since the bombs fell, many people have questioned whether the United States truly needed to unleash such a devastating weapon, arguing that Japan was already prepared to surrender. Four years after the bomb was dropped, Hanson W. Baldwin published *Great Mistakes of the War*, lamenting that: "It is my contention that in the eyes of the world the atomic bomb has cost us dearly; we have lost morally; we no longer are the world's moral leader."[8]

From World War to Cold War

Truman was now a peacetime president, but it was an anxious peace. The beginning of the Cold War between the United States and the Soviet Union marked the next seven-and-a-half years of Truman's presidency. The conflict would shape not only his foreign policy decisions, but his domestic agenda as well.

Although the United States and the Soviet Union had been allies in World War II, tension had existed between the two superpowers as early as 1917. Even during World War II, they disagreed over the future of Poland—Soviet leader Joseph Stalin had set up a pro-communist government there, following the Soviet troops' victory over Germany, and believed, unlike the other allies, that Poland should be under Soviet control. Stalin's leadership was in general a great concern to Western leaders such as Truman, Roosevelt, and Churchill, all of whom—while acknowledging that Stalin could be quite personable—believed him to be a very dangerous dictator. Churchill expressed his concerns about the Soviets in a speech he gave in March 1946, when he declared that an "iron curtain" had fallen between the democracies of Western Europe and the Soviet-controlled nations of Eastern Europe. During the previous month, George Kennan, who was the chargé d'affaires at the U.S. embassy in Mosow, transmitted what came to be known as the "Long Telegram." Kennan declared that the United States could not expect to have reasonable relations with the Soviet Union and should instead be committed to confronting the actions of the Soviets and containing their power. He wrote in the telegram: "Soviet power . . . does not work by fixed plans. It does not take unnecessary risks.

Impervious to logic of reason, it is highly sensitive to logic of force. For this reason it can easily withdraw . . . when strong resistance is encountered at any point."[9]

The Truman Doctrine and the Marshall Plan

Between 1944 and 1947, communist governments were established in Albania, Yugoslavia, Romania, Bulgaria, Hungary, and Poland. While these were all Eastern European nations, concerns were growing that communism was presenting a threat to Western Europe. Greece was embroiled in a civil war against communist forces, while Turkey's government was refusing to make concessions to the Soviets. In a speech before Congress on March 12, 1947, Truman stated that these nations, and free nations in general, needed American aid in order to ensure stable democracies. This policy would become known as the Truman Doctrine. As the president explained to Congress:

> I believe that it must be the policy of the United States to support free peoples who are resisting attempted subjugation by armed minorities or by outside pressures.
>
> I believe that we must assist free peoples to work out their own destinies in their own way.
>
> I believe that our help should be primarily through economic and financial aid which is essential to economic stability and orderly political processes.[10]

Congress approved a $400 million aid package for Greece and Turkey, which Truman signed into law on March 22, 1947. The civil war in Greece ended in 1949 with the defeat of the communists, and Turkey continued to withstand Soviet pressures.

Greece and Turkey were not alone in needing help. World War II had devastated Europe; bombed buildings cluttered the landscape and the continent was struggling to rebuild its economy. A drought in 1946 had caused a severe food shortage, and industrial production in 1947 was less than two-thirds the normal peacetime rate. The European economies also suffered from inflated currency and trade imbalances. The United States had already provided more than $9 billion in aid programs to Europe since the war's end, but it had not been sufficient.

With those concerns in mind, the U.S. State Department tried to develop a way to assist the nations of Western Europe. Under the leadership of George C. Marshall—a general who had served as U.S. Army chief of staff in World War II and was now Truman's secretary of state—reports were written by undersecretary of state and economic affairs William L. Clayton and Kennan during the spring of 1947. These reports concluded that "the revival of a politically and economically stable Europe also would mean more security and economic well-being for the United States."[11]

Discussions on how to revive Europe's economy continued through the spring. Marshall was asked during that time to give the commencement speech at Harvard University. With the help of state department employee Charles Bohlen, he wrote an address that combined elements from Clayton's and Kennan's reports and added some of his own views. On June 5, 1947, Marshall told the audience about the dangers that faced Europe and what America needed to do to help:

> The truth of the matter is that Europe's requirements for the next three or four years of foreign food and other essential products—principally from America—are so much greater than her present ability to pay that she must have substantial additional help or face economic, social, and political deterioration of a very grave character.
>
> The remedy lies in breaking the vicious cycle and restoring the confidence of the European people in the

economic future of their own countries and of Europe as a whole. . . .

It is logical that the United States should do whatever it is able to do to assist in the return of normal economic health in the world, without which there can be no political stability and no assured peace.[12]

Marshall called on the nations of Europe to help in the development of the assistance program. The Soviet Union was involved in the initial process but withdrew their delegation because they believed Marshall's plan threatened their sovereignty. Representatives from the United States and sixteen Western European nations met in Paris in July 1947 to begin the formulation of the program. Truman spoke in front of Congress on December 19, 1947, to urge approval of the Economic Co-operation Act, which would oversee the European Recovery Program, more commonly known as the Marshall Plan. The act became law on April 3, 1948.

The United States provided more than $13.5 billion in aid over the next three years, the bulk of it in food and agricultural supplies, along with fuel, vehicles, and machinery. More than half a billion dollars of private relief parcels were also sent to Europe. The impact on Europe was tremendous. In his book *The Marshall Plan, 1947–1951*, Theodore A. Wilson writes: "The effects on Europe's economic vitality were striking. Industrial production in Western Europe in 1950 was 45 percent higher than in 1947. . . . By 1952 European industries were churning out goods at a rate of 200 percent above that in 1938."[13] Marshall's efforts earned him the 1953 Nobel Peace Prize.

The Berlin Airlift and the Formation of NATO

The United States' humanitarian efforts in Europe—and its conflicts with the Soviet Union—were not limited to the Marshall Plan. In March 1948, the United States,

Britain, and France decided to unify the sectors they controlled in Berlin. The Soviets responded on June 24 by declaring that the Allies no longer had power in Berlin and beginning a blockade between Berlin and the West that prevented automobiles and trains from entering or leaving the city. Without aid, the residents of Berlin faced a complete depletion of their food supply by August. Truman had to decide how to answer the USSR's actions. Although he considered a military response, the president instead authorized an airlift that would bring food, coal, and other essentials into the beleaguered city. The Berlin airlift began on June 26, 1948, and was led by General Lucius D. Clay and Lieutenant Curtis LeMay, with planes flown by the U.S. Air Force, the British Royal Air Force, and civilians. The airlift lasted until September 1949, though the Soviets backed down and lifted the blockade in May. All told, the planes carried more than 1.5 million tons of coal, over a half-million tons of food, and 92,282 tons of petroleum products. Truman wrote in his memoirs that the airlift "demonstrated to the people of Europe that with their cooperation we would act, and act resolutely, when their freedom was threatened."[14] Such humanitarianism did not come without a price, however: Sixty pilots and five Germans died during the airlift.

Another response to concerns over Soviet threats was the formation of the North Atlantic Treaty Organization in 1949 by the United States, Canada, Belgium, Denmark, France, Great Britain, Iceland, Italy, Luxembourg, the Netherlands, Norway, and Portugal. Although it was intended to encourage social, political, and economic cooperation, the centerpiece of NATO was the pledge that all members would respond if any of the twelve nations were attacked. The United States had earlier become a member of another international organization in July 1945, after the Senate approved the charter of the United Nations.

The United States also aided Japan in its rebuilding, although that process was more political than humanitarian in nature. General Douglas MacArthur, who had led campaigns in the Pacific throughout World War II, was named commander of the Allied powers in Japan and was responsible for the Allied occupation following Japan's surrender. The main accomplishments of MacArthur's command were the revision of Japan's constitution, which made the emperor a symbolic leader with no political power, and the expansion of the political and civil liberties of its citizens.

The Korean War

Asia also presented the United States with more concerns about communism. The Chinese Communist Party had been founded in 1921. Twenty-eight years later, the Communists controlled the entire Chinese mainland, prompting Chiang Kai-shek, who had been the leader of the Nationalist government since 1928, to flee to Taiwan. Another communist nation was established in 1948 when Korea was split into two countries—the democratic Republic of Korea in the south and the communist Democratic People's Republic in the north.

North Korean forces invaded South Korea on June 25, 1950. Two days later, concerned that South Korea could fall to communist forces, Truman authorized the use of American military forces in Korea; the following month, he appointed MacArthur to lead the American and United Nations troops. Because Truman had not officially declared war, controversy followed as to whether the fighting could be considered a war or a "police action."

The Korean War lasted for three years, ending on July 27, 1953, six months after Truman's presidency ended. Although the war was a stalemate for the most part, the United States had an important victory early on at Inchon. MacArthur oversaw the campaign, an amphibious assault on September 15, 1950. Eighty thousand Marines and 261 ships came on shore with few casualties. The Marines reached and recaptured Seoul at month's end and by early October had driven the North Korean troops out of South Korea.

Although MacArthur had some success in Korea, he and the president were constantly at odds over how best to approach the war. Truman desired a limited war, with the goal of defending the positions of the American and U.N. troops. MacArthur, on the other hand, sought all-out victory and wanted to bring the war to the Chinese mainland. Truman disagreed, fearing that expansion could lead to a full-scale war with the Soviet Union. The battle between the general and the president peaked in spring 1951. MacArthur put American plans for negotiation at risk that spring when he warned China to admit defeat or face a possible invasion. On April 5, a letter MacArthur had written to Speaker of the House Joseph Martin, criticizing the administration's foreign policy, became public. Faced with MacArthur's insubordination, Truman dismissed the general on April 11.

It was one of the president's least popular decisions. MacArthur was greeted with parades upon his return to the United States, while Truman was burned in effigy. The *Congressional Record* of that year is filled with outrage about the president's actions. Kentucky congressman James S. Golden declared that no one could take the place of MacArthur and labeled Truman's decision the act of a "weak and impetuous man."[15] Hearings held in May gave MacArthur the opportunity to explain his views on the war, and congressional support for the general remained high. However, many politicians and military analysts argued that the president was obligated to dismiss MacArthur—because the U.S. military is ultimately under civilian control—and eventually public opinion turned in favor of Truman. Matthew B. Ridgway, the man who replaced MacArthur in Korea, wrote an account of the war where he reiterated the importance of civilian control. According to Ridgway: "If the President had failed—after

MacArthur's repeated neglect to comply with directives and after the General's public airing of displeasure with approved government policies—to relieve MacArthur from duty, he would have been derelict in his own duty."[16]

Recognizing Israel

Not every foreign policy decision that Truman made was in response to communism. The decision to recognize the new country of Israel was probably the most prominent example. The campaign to establish a Jewish nation had begun in 1897, when Theodore Herzl convened the first Zionist Congress. The goal of Herzl and his fellow Zionists was to create a home for Jews in Palestine. Great Britain expressed their support for this goal in 1917 with the issuing of the Balfour Declaration, but in 1939 placed restrictions on the immigration of Jews to Palestine. By that point, the Nazi persecution of German Jews was well underway. Despite Great Britain's immigration restrictions, the Jewish community brought 85,000 Holocaust survivors into Palestine between 1945 and 1948. The issue of what to do about Palestine was considered by the United Nations in 1947; on November 25, the organization decided to partition Palestine—which would be under Great Britain's mandate until the following May—into Jewish and Arab sections. On May 14, 1948, Jewish authorities established the state of Israel.

In the months preceding the declaration, Truman and his administration debated if and when the United States should recognize the new nation. The president had earlier shown sympathy to the plight of European Jews. Richard Lawrence Miller notes that Senator Truman was a member of the American Palestine Committee and also supported the United Palestine Appeal, an organization that helped European Jews settle in Palestine. The senator gave a speech in April 1943 where he discussed the slaughter of the Jews and concluded: "We must do all that is humanly possible to provide a haven and place of safety for all those who can be grasped from the hands of the Nazi butchers. . . . This is not a Jewish problem. It is an American problem."[17]

However, Truman was not initially supportive of a Jewish nation. Before the United Nations ordered the partition of Palestine, Truman had wished for Jews and Arabs to rule together, but he did tell the American U.N. delegation to vote for partition. That decision was not popular among many of his top advisers, particularly Marshall, who believed that America could face long-range problems if it supported Zionism. Eddie Jacobson, Truman's longtime friend and former business partner, urged the president to

recognize Israel. On May 12, Truman aide Clark Clifford said that because they had already supported partition, the United States had no choice but to recognize the Jewish state as soon as it was established. Truman followed Clifford's advice. A mere eleven minutes after Israel declared its independence, the United States became the first country to officially recognize the new nation.

The Fair Deal

Although foreign concerns dominated much of Truman's presidency, domestic issues also played an important role. Truman was charged with the responsibility of bringing the nation into a peacetime economy; the United States could no longer depend on wartime industries. The centerpiece of Truman's domestic policy was known as the Fair Deal. It was Truman's effort to expand on Franklin Roosevelt's New Deal—the series of programs enacted to lift the country out of the Great Depression in the 1930s. Truman laid out his domestic agenda in a September 6, 1945, address to Congress. He called for a higher minimum wage, an increase in Social Security benefits, wage and price controls to slow inflation, and a national health insurance program, among other things.

Truman had several successes, with Congress approving his public housing bill and passing laws that expanded Social Security and increased the minimum wage. However, Congress largely ignored Truman's desire to slow inflation, instead choosing to approve a tax-relief package. Truman's efforts to see much of the Fair Deal become law were stymied by the 1946 midterm elections, in which the Republicans gained control of both houses of Congress. The Democrats regained both houses in 1948, but they lost most of their majority in the 1950 elections. Consequently, Truman lacked a strongly liberal Democratic majority to support his agenda.

Among the failures of the Fair Deal was the Brannan

Plan. Designed by Truman adviser Charles Brannan, it was intended to protect farmers by setting an upper limit on production and providing direct payments in order to maintain their income. Brannan campaigned extensively for the plan, and it had considerable liberal support, but the increasingly conservative political atmosphere that had resulted from the Korean War led to the plan's failure to become law. Despite the disappointments of the Fair Deal, Truman scholar Alonzo Hamby maintains that "Truman, whatever his inadequacies, was the foremost spokesman of American liberalism."[18]

The President's Committee on Civil Rights

Civil rights were another important part of Truman's domestic agenda. Truman's commitment to civil rights was especially interesting because Truman's private views toward minorities were not particularly tolerant. His mother, who died in 1947 at the age of 94 and was a staunch Confederate during the Civil War, might have influenced the president's attitudes. He often traded racist jokes with his colleagues and considered blacks to be inferior to whites. As Truman biographer Richard Lawrence Miller notes:

> Truman's prejudice makes his civil rights record all the more remarkable. It is one thing to favor civil rights because one believes in racial equality and integration. Truman promoted civil rights despite his dislike of blacks and his possible feeling that they were inferior humans. This shows not only a genuine tolerance for others but a firm belief in the idea of America as a land of opportunity. Truman believed that inferiors had a right to seek the good life even if they lacked the inherent ability to achieve it.[19]

Seeking information on the extent of discrimination in the United States, Truman appointed a President's Committee on Civil Rights in December 1946. The committee, whose members included business and labor leaders, lawyers, clergymen, and two African Americans, issued a report the following October, *To Secure These Rights.* The report detailed the barriers facing minorities in education and work and offered suggestions to reduce discrimination. Truman gave an address to Congress on February 2, 1948, in which he urged the legislature to enact many of the committee's recommendations, such as passing an anti-lynching law and establishing a permanent Fair Employment Practices Commission. Congress largely ignored his agenda, so he turned to executive orders. On July 26, 1948, he issued two orders—one to desegregate the military, the other to ban discrimination in the federal civil service. While Truman did not completely succeed in improving the situation for minorities—either because opposition to civil rights was too strong or because Truman did not make enough use of his executive powers—he did, as history professor William E. Leuchtenburg has written, "[make] civil rights a proper concern for the national government, and for the first time ever the Democratic party became the main protagonist for the rights of blacks."[20]

In the midst of his civil rights agenda, Truman was also dealing with a difficult presidential campaign. He was considered an underdog in 1948 to New York governor Thomas E. Dewey. Not only was Dewey popular but Truman also faced opposition from the Dixiecrats, Southern Democrats who opposed Truman's civil rights agenda. The Dixiecrats nominated South Carolina governor Strom Thurmond for the presidency and threatened to siphon most of the South's votes; as it turned out, Thurmond won four states in that region, but Truman took the rest. Despite the obstacles, including polls and magazine articles that expressed the commonly held view that Truman would lose, Truman campaigned relentlessly and gave speeches throughout the country. But on the morning after the election, despite the predictions, Dewey called Truman to concede. A photograph of Truman holding a copy of the *Chicago Daily Tri-*

bune with the erroneous headline "Dewey Defeats Truman"—printed before Truman took the lead in the election in the early morning—became one of the most famous in American political history.

The Rise of Anti-Communism

With the start of the Cold War, U.S. leaders became suspicious of communist sympathizers and worried that communist agents were trying to infiltrate the government. The president issued an executive order in March 1947 outlining procedures to ensure that all government employees were loyal to the United States. American writer Whittaker Chambers testified in 1948 that he had been a member of the Communist Party in the 1920s and 1930s and had helped send secret messages to the Soviets. He also alleged that Alger Hiss, an employee at the State Department, was a Communist. Hiss denied the charges but was eventually convicted for perjury in January 1950.

Wisconsin senator Joseph R. McCarthy was a central figure in the growing "Red Scare." He gave a speech on February 9, 1950, where he declared that 205 Communists were working in the state department. Eleven days later he made a speech where he reduced the number of alleged Communists to fifty-seven but still made clear that he thought the United States faced a serious internal risk. According to McCarthy: "We are not dealing with spies who get 30 pieces of silver to steal the blueprints of a new weapon. We are dealing with a far more sinister type of activity because it permits the enemy to guide and shape our policy."[21]

The fears raised by McCarthy and other congressmen, such as California senator Richard Nixon, led to the passage of the McCarran Act, or the Internal Security Act of 1950. The act placed travel and employment restrictions on known Communists and required communist organizations to register with the U.S. attorney general. Truman vetoed the bill, arguing that it posed a threat to freedom of expression, but the veto was overridden. McCarthy was discredited in hearings held in 1954 but the damage he did to the American political system was significant.

Developing a Postwar Economy

In addition to worries about communism, a recurring problem during the Truman administration was the conflict between unions and big business. Strikes were rampant in 1946, as workers from the steel industry, General Motors, the United Mine Workers, meatpackers, telephone workers, and several other industries walked off their jobs. One potentially devastating strike was that of the railroad workers. Truman signed an executive order on May 17, 1946, the day before the strike was due to begin, giving the government the power to seize and operate the railroads. His action led to a five-day postponement of the strike. When it began on May 23, the strike led to a virtual standstill of the railroad system; nearly 200,000 freight and passenger trains stopped running. The next day, after receiving numerous telegrams detailing the ways the strike was affecting the nation, from stranded passengers to panics over food shortages, the president spoke to the nation and said that if the railroad workers did not end their strike, he would be obliged to call out the Army. The following afternoon, Truman declared that all workers on strike would be drafted into the military. During the speech, Truman learned that the railroad strike had ended.

Congress responded to the myriad strikes by passing the Taft-Hartley bill, which had been crafted by Senator Robert A. Taft (the son of President William Howard Taft) and Representative Fred Hartley. The act gave the government the power to place an eighty-day injunction on strikes it deemed a threat to national safety, forbade unions to contribute to political campaigns, outlawed union-only workplaces, banned union tactics such as secondary boycotts, and required that union officers file affidavits that they were not Communists. Truman vetoed the bill on the grounds that it would lead to the loss of protections for workers but was overridden on June 23, 1947.

Another strike played an important role in the waning months of the Truman presidency. Steelworkers, angry that they had not received a pay raise since 1950, were intending to go on strike on April 8, 1952. Truman was concerned that a strike would prevent the production of needed weapons and ammunitions, so on the day the workers planned to walk off their jobs, he declared that the government was seizing the steel mills. He chose that route rather than utilizing the powers in the Taft-Hartley Act that would have delayed the strike for eighty days. His decision was immediately controversial—some congressmen called for his impeachment and the media questioned whether Truman would one day seize newspapers the way he had the steel mills. The steel industry sued to regain control of the plants and the case reached the Supreme Court. The court ruled 6–3 against Truman on June 2, declaring that he did not have the authority to take control of private property. A fifty-three-day strike followed; it cost $400 million in lost wages and 21 million tons in lost production, including one-third of the military output. The entire episode was one of the most difficult of Truman's presidency. He expressed his disappointment in his memoirs, noting that the government had seized strike-threatened plants in the past and arguing, "In this day and age the defense of the nation means more than building an army, navy, and air force. . . . The President, who is Commander in Chief and who represents the interest of all the people, must be able to act at all times to meet any sudden threat to the nation's security."[22]

Leaving the White House

In 1951, Congress passed the twenty-third amendment, which limited a president to a total of ten years in office and no more than two terms. Although the amendment did not apply to the current resident of the White House,

Truman chose not to run for reelection in 1952. He had announced the decision to his staff in November 1951, explaining in a memorandum: "I know I could be reelected again and continue to break the old precedent that was broken by FDR. It should not be done. That precedent should continue . . . by custom based on the honor of the man in the office."[23] He made his decision public in a March 29, 1952, speech at a Democratic fundraiser.

At the Democratic national convention that year, Illinois governor Adlai Stevenson won the nomination for president. He was defeated in the general election by Republican candidate and World War II hero General Dwight D. Eisenhower. After twenty years, the Republicans had regained the White House.

By 1953, Truman had spent nearly thirty consecutive years in public life, including eighteen years in Washington. He and his family returned to Independence, Missouri. Truman published his memoirs in 1955 and 1956 and attended the dedication of the Truman Library—also in Independence—in July 1957. Truman spent much of his time at the library for the next ten years, but by that point his health had begun failing, beginning with a fall in his bathroom in 1964. On December 5, 1972, suffering from lung congestion, he was taken to Kansas City's Research Hospital and Medical Center. Over the next three weeks, Truman's heart, lungs, and digestive system began to fail, and he fell into a coma on Christmas Day. On December 26, 1972, the thirty-third president of the United States died. He was buried in the courtyard of his library. Bess Truman died ten years later and was buried next to her husband.

"The Buck Stops Here"

At first glance, Harry S. Truman might seem like an unlikely man to have led the United States through the end of World War II and the beginning of the Cold War. He was a failed businessman who never attended college and who entered politics fairly late in life. He lacked the political brilliance of Franklin D. Roosevelt or Winston Churchill; he also was not as obviously charismatic as Douglas MacArthur. And yet, Truman succeeded in establishing America as a superpower—one whose chief responsibilities include humanitarian efforts towards nations in political and economic need—and eventually earned respect from both political parties as one of the nation's greatest presidents.

Truman famously had a placard on his desk that read "The buck stops here." He made controversial decisions—dropping the bombs on Japan, dismissing MacArthur—and did not back down from the criticism he received. But Truman was also willing to listen to other points of view before he made those decisions, and he surrounded himself with men well qualified to offer advice, such as George Marshall and Dean Acheson, who both served as secretary of state. Truman did not spurn the opinions of his cabinet and other officials because he did not see himself as being above others. As Ferrell writes: "If a single trait could be credited with making Truman a great president, it was his modesty. . . . He carefully drew a distinction between himself and the office."[24] Ferrell credits Truman's Baptist faith and the influence of his wife and daughter with keeping Truman humble. Ken Hechler, who worked as Truman's research director in the White House, concludes in his memoirs that what made Truman a great president was "that he never lost the common touch and was determined to use the awesome power of the presidency to help bring peace and justice to the average people all over the world."[25]

Notes

1. Robert Ferrell, *Harry S. Truman and the Modern American Presidency*. Boston: Little, Brown, and Co., 1983, p. 6.
2. Quoted in David McCullough, *Truman*. New York: Simon & Schuster, 1992, p. 118.
3. McCullough, *Truman*, p. 153.

4. McCullough, *Truman*, p. 156.

5. Richard Lawrence Miller, *Truman: The Rise to Power*. New York: McGraw-Hill, 1986, pp. 260–261.

6. Margaret Truman, *Harry S. Truman*. New York: William Morrow, 1973, p. 65.

7. McCullough, *Truman*, p. 265.

8. Hanson W. Baldwin, *Great Mistakes of the War*. New York: Harper and Brothers, 1949, p. 92.

9. Telegram from George Kennan, February 22, 1946.

10. President Truman's address to Congress, March 12, 1947.

11. James T. Gay, "Rebuilding Europe," *American History*, May/June 1947.

12. George C. Marshall, address at Harvard University, June 5, 1947.

13. Theodore A. Wilson, *The Marshall Plan: 1947–1951*. New York: Foreign Policy Association, 1977, p. 47.

14. Harry S. Truman, *Memoirs by Harry S. Truman, Volume Two: Years of Trial and Hope, 1946–1952*. Garden City, NY: Doubleday, 1955, p. 131.

15. James S. Golden, remarks in the *Congressional Record*, April 12, 1951, p. A1991.

16. Matthew B. Ridgway, *The Korean War*. Garden City, NY: Doubleday, 1967, p. 236.

17. Miller, *Truman: The Rise to Power*, pp. 390–391.

18. Alonzo Hamby, *Beyond the New Deal: Harry S. Truman and American Liberalism*. New York: Columbia University Press, 1973, p. 350.

19. Miller, *Truman: The Rise to Power*, p. 327.

20. William E. Leuchtenburg, "The Conversion of Harry Truman," *American Heritage*, November 1991, p. 68.

21. Joseph R. McCarthy, remarks in the *Congressional Record*, February 20, 1950, pp. 1954–57.

22. Harry S. Truman, *Memoirs by Harry S. Truman, Volume Two*, p. 478.

23. Margaret Truman, *Harry S. Truman*, p. 527.

24. Ferrell, *Harry S. Truman and the Modern American Presidency*, p. 180.

25. Ken Hechler, *Working with Truman: A Personal Memoir of the White House Years*. New York: Putnam, 1982, p. 283.

CHAPTER

1

DROPPING THE ATOMIC BOMB ON JAPAN

Truman's Military Experience Helped Shape His Decision to Drop the Bomb

Alonzo L. Hamby

President Truman was a soldier during World War I and experienced the dangers and devastations of war firsthand. Alonzo L. Hamby writes that those experiences, along with the advice of Truman's top advisers, led the president to his decision to drop atomic bombs on Japan during World War II. After consulting with men such as Secretary of War Henry L. Stimson, Truman concluded that there was no other way to bring about Japan's unconditional surrender. Hamby believes that Truman was justified in his decision. Hamby is a professor of history at Ohio University in Athens, Ohio, and the author of *Man of the People: A Life of Harry S. Truman.*

H ARRY S. TRUMAN HAD BEEN PRESIDENT OF THE UNITED States for less than two weeks on April 25th, 1945, when Secretary of War Henry L. Stimson delivered to him a full report on the most expensive and secret American enterprise of the Second World War. The document began with the chilling words, 'Within four months, we shall in

From "Truman and the Bomb," by Alonzo Hamby, *History Today*, August 1995. Reprinted by permission of *History Today*.

all probability have completed the most terrible weapon ever known in human history'. From that point until he received word of its successful test in mid-July, the atomic bomb was at the back of Truman's mind as he attempted to cope with the manifold problems accompanying the end of the greatest war in human history.

On May 8th, Truman's sixty-first birthday, Germany surrendered unconditionally. It was still necessary to achieve final victory in the Pacific and manage a multitude of diplomatic difficulties with the Allies, especially the Soviet Union, not yet at war with Japan and (so it seemed) desperately needed for the final campaigns in the Pacific conflict.

Truman's Personal Attitudes Towards War

Truman's attitude to the war was heavily motivated by his own experience as a combat artilleryman in the First World War, in his perceptions of Japanese fanaticism, and in forming his identity as a politician attempting to establish the limits of his discretion. Revisionist scholars, motivated by a pacifist revulsion against the horrors of nuclear war, have criticised his eventual use of the atomic bomb as unnecessary; some have asserted that he cynically sacrificed Japanese lives in an effort to intimidate the Soviet Union. Such charges have little merit. An examination of the available evidence, considered within the context of 1945 rather than 1995, reveals a president who made imperfect judgements and was shaken by the destruction he wrought, but who could rightly think he was acting simply to end a terrible war being fought against an implacable enemy.

Diplomatic issues stemming from the termination of the European war and the establishment of the United Nations necessarily occupied much of Truman's attention during his first three months in office, but the struggle against Japan was never far from his attention. On April 1st, just eleven days before he took office, American troops had landed on Okinawa, 400 miles from the southernmost

Japanese island of Kyushu. Allied forces, mostly American but including a British naval contingent, had overwhelming superiority. Okinawa was smaller than Rhode Island: nevertheless, the battle that followed lasted nearly three months. More than 100,000 Japanese troops defended the island, fighting with suicidal tenacity. Waves of kamikaze planes attacked the American fleet, inflicting greater losses than the Japanese navy had managed over the past year.

As Truman read daily battle reports, he surely thought of his own combat experiences and of those of his close friends in the Argonne area and then to the east of Verdun during the Great War: finding himself in NoMan's Land while acting as a forward observer for his artillery regiment; his cousin, Captain Ralph Truman, pulling a shattered infantry force together against a German counterattack; Major John Miles, a close comrade, holding his artillery battalion firm in the same action; corpses along dusty roads; a dying freckle-faced kid with a leg blown off; the scattered remains of unknown soldiers heaved from shallow graves by German artillery shells. And he must have thought of two friends who had served under him in that war, Eddie McKim and Abie Burkhart, both of whom had already lost sons in the current war. And he surely thought of his four nephews, all of them in uniform, one of them a sailor on the USS *Missouri*, off Okinawa.

The Role of the Interim Committee

Despite his willingness to assume full and sole responsibility for use of the atomic bomb in later years, Truman dealt with the impending event in the fashion of a circumspect chairman of the board. He appointed a committee. Headed by Stimson and containing James Byrnes (soon to be appointed Secretary of State) as his personal representative, the Interim Committee, as it was called, saw the bomb, however terrible, as a proxy for the thousand-plane raids that had already devastated numerous German and

Japanese cities. None of the committee members, scientists and politicians alike, fully understood the horrifying radioactive side-effects of nuclear warfare. On June 1st, citing all the uncertainties of employing an unprecedented (and as yet untested) weapon, the Interim Committee recommended use of the bomb against Japan without warning. No one doubted that Truman would accept the advice.

On June 18th, the president met with his top military officials to discuss the possible scenarios for ending the war against Japan. They recommended an invasion of Kyushu no later than November 1st. The operation would be enormous: 766,000 American assault troops engaging an estimated 350,000 Japanese defenders. It would be followed in 1946 by a decisive campaign near Tokyo on the main island of Honshu.

Would the Kyushu operation, Truman asked, be 'another Okinawa closer to Japan'? With questionable optimism, the military chiefs of staff predicted the casualties would be somewhat lighter. Still their estimate for the first thirty days was 31,000 casualties. Truman gave his reluctant approval, but not without saying he hoped 'there was a possibility of preventing an Okinawa from one end of Japan to another'. In fact, Pentagon planners were at work on estimates that projected 132,000 casualties (killed, wounded, missing) for Kyushu, another 90,000 or so for Honshu. Of these, probably a quarter would be fatalities. The figures were not wholly worked out by the June 18th meeting but they would be given to Truman in due course and would constitute the estimates upon which he acted. In later years, he exaggerated them, but they required no magnification to make the atomic bomb a compelling option.

Debating Alternatives to the Bomb

The June 18th meeting also explored ways in which the war might be concluded without either the Kyushu invasion or the atomic bomb. Should the United States, could

Truman appointed a committee, headed by Secretary of War Henry L. Stimson (pictured right), to advise him on the use of the atomic bomb.

it, accept less than unconditional surrender from Japan? The president's personal military chief of staff, Admiral William D. Leahy, was most emphatic in asserting that it should. Transfixed by the fanaticism of Japanese resistance, fearful that American losses would exceed Pentagon estimates, doubtful that the bomb would ever work, Leahy declared that Japan could not menace the United States in the foreseeable future. Stimson and Assistant Secretary of War John J. McCloy favoured giving the Japanese guarantees that they could keep the emperor.

Truman appeared somewhat sympathetic, said he had left the door open for Congress to alter the unconditional surrender policy, but felt he could not take action to change public opinion. He apparently did not believe that an utterly defeated Japan might be allowed to retain the emperor under terms that still could be called 'unconditional surrender' and that the American people would prefer so minor a compromise to another year of war.

Should the United States warn the Japanese of its atomic capability, perhaps even arrange some sort of demonstration? McCloy alone argued for doing so. Other military leaders argued the shock value of surprise. The Interim Committee had explicitly rejected such proposals. Byrnes, who was formally named Secretary of State on July 3rd, strongly favoured both rigid unconditional surrender and total surprise.

Truman had been presented with a wide consensus from an interlocking directorate composed of the men who had won the war: the Interim Committee, his top military leaders, and his most important Cabinet members. He would feel a need to talk of using the atomic bomb against strictly military targets, but that, which he probably realised was not realistic, was his only inhibition.

The four weeks after June 18th were intensely busy for the new president. In addition to a budget message for Congress, he faced a wide range of military and diplomatic matters—the San Francisco conference to establish the United Nations, myriad conflicts with the Soviet Union in occupied Germany and Eastern Europe, numerous squabbles with the French and British, the shape of the post-war Far East. Above all, so long as the atomic bomb remained a prospect, rather than an accomplished reality, he had to nail down Soviet participation in the war against Japan.

Many of these issues came to a head when he met at Potsdam with [Soviet leader Joseph] Stalin and [British prime minister Winston] Churchill. (Near the end of the conference, after the Conservative election defeat, Clement Attlee replaced Churchill.) Truman arrived on July 15th; the conference would last until August 2nd. During his time away from the negotiations—his spare time, astonishingly—he would grapple with the bomb as an actuality and make the final decisions required.

On July 15th, Truman toured the rubble of Berlin. 'What a pity that the human animal is not able to put his moral thinking into practice!' he mused. 'I fear that machines are ahead of morals by some centuries'. Perhaps thinking of the bomb, he added, 'we are only termites on a planet and maybe when we bore too deeply into the planet there'll be a reckoning—who knows?'

He may well have written those lines after meeting between 7.30 and 8.00 PM with Secretary Stimson, who presented him with a top secret message he had just received from his closest aide, George Harrison. Tersely and obliquely, it indicated that the first atomic test, near Alamogordo in the New Mexico desert, had been a great success. On the morning of July 18th, Stimson gave Truman another message from Harrison in Washington: the flash of the explosion had been visible for 250 miles, the sound of the blast had carried 50 miles. Truman, Stimson wrote in his diary, was 'highly delighted . . . evidently very greatly reinforced'.

Truman confided some thoughts to his own diary that day. Since they have been badly distorted by at least one writer, they are worth quoting in full:

> Discussed Manhattan (it is a success). Decided to tell Stalin about it. Stalin had told PM [Churchill] of telegram from Jap Emperor asking for peace. Stalin also read his answer to me. It was satisfactory. Believe Japs will fold up before Russia comes in.

> I am sure they will when Manhattan appears over their homeland. I shall inform Stalin about it at an opportune time. . . .

Selecting a Target

The bomb had given Truman a sense of enormous power. At a stroke, it had changed his position from that of a supplicant in quest of an ally against Japan to a more-than-equal partner now able to be indifferent. Churchill had observed on July 21st that the president was markedly more assertive and considerably firmer in rejecting Soviet demands. Now he understood why. A consensus quickly developed among the British and Americans that the USSR should be told as little as possible. On July 24th, at the conclusion of the day's negotiations, Truman walked over to Stalin and, as he later would tell it, 'casually mentioned . . . that we had a new weapon of unusual destructive force'.

Stalin, poker-faced, said that he hoped the United States would make good use of it, asked no questions, and made no further comments. Of course, thanks to his espionage ring at Los Alamos, he was actually well-informed about the Manhattan Project, although he may not yet have learned of the successful test. The Americans, many of them puzzled at his lack of interest, did not realise that they had witnessed the first display of an interim Soviet strategy for dealing with the bomb—to behave as if it were irrelevant—until the USSR could produce one of its own.

As Truman remembered it in 1952, he asked his top advisers once again about likely casualties in the planned invasions of Kyushu and Honshu and received from General George Marshall an estimate of about 250,000 Americans and at least an equal number of Japanese. Of those with whom he talked, no one was more important than Stimson, who had his total respect and was directly responsible for the atomic project.

When Stimson insisted on dropping Kyoto from the target list, Truman concurred (in Stimson's words) 'with the utmost emphasis'. The military saw Kyoto as a prime industrial target; Stimson saw it as a city of shrines and cultural centres that could not be destroyed without alienating the Japanese population. Stimson was probably also the key figure, if only through his silence, in leading Truman to accept a strategy of dropping the first two bombs in rapid succession. The idea was to convince the Japanese that the United States had a large stockpile.

As to use of the bomb, there was no dissent among the primary advisers. On July 25th, Truman gave the final go-ahead. Sometime during the first ten days of August, the bomb would be used against Hiroshima, Kokura, or Nigata in that order of choice—unless Japan surrendered unconditionally.

Japan Refuses to Surrender

On July 26th, the United States, Great Britain and China issued a proclamation from Potsdam demanding the unconditional surrender of Japan. The alternative would be 'the inevitable and complete destruction of the Japanese armed forces and . . . the utter devastation of the Japanese homeland'. Following the decisions already made in Washington, the ultimatum did not mention an atomic bomb. Nor did it specifically state that Japan would be allowed to retain the emperor; instead, it promised to recognise 'in accordance with the freely expressed will of the Japanese people a peacefully inclined and responsible government'.

On July 28th, Japan rejected the proclamation with a verb that could be translated as 'treat with silent contempt' or 'ignore entirely'. The government, Prime Minister [Kantaro] Suzuki asserted, would 'resolutely fight for the successful conclusion of this war'.

For most Americans, 'unconditional surrender' had become a wartime objective carved in stone; having obtained it from Germany, no American president could appear to negotiate anything less with Japan, which in turn surely bore the burden of responsibility for ending a war it had started. Still, the United States could have made it clear, either publicly or through diplomatic backchannels, that unconditional surrender would not mean removal of the emperor. Whether Japan would have responded to such an initiative cannot be known, but one can only regret that it did not crystallise in Truman's mind before the obliteration of two cities.

As it was, the president allowed things to go forward, buoyed by a belief that the war would soon be ended without a massive invasion, yet not entirely comfortable with what he had done. Writing in his diary, he portrayed his orders to Stimson in terms that in his heart he had to know were unrealistic:

> I have told the Sec. of War, Mr Stimson, to use it so that military objectives and soldiers and sailors are the target and not women and children. Even if the Japs are savages, ruthless, merciless and fanatic, we as the leader of the world for the common welfare cannot drop this terrible bomb on the old Capitol [Kyoto] or the new [Tokyo].
>
> He & I are in accord. The target will be a purely military one . . .

At approximately 8.11 AM on August 6th, a B-29, the *Enola Gay*, piloted by Colonel Paul Tibbets, dropped an atomic bomb over the city of Hiroshima from an altitude of 31,600 feet. The explosion occurred at 2,000 feet. Observers in a trailing B-29 witnessed the blinding fireball, the shock wave, the mushroom cloud rising miles into the sky. The central city, built on a level plain, was instantly in flames; almost nothing remained standing within a one-mile radius of 'ground zero'. Perhaps 75,000 people, mostly civilians, were killed at once; more tens of thousands would eventually die from the effects of radiation. No single device in the history of warfare had killed so many people so indiscriminately.

The news reached Truman as he was returning from Potsdam aboard the cruiser *Augusta*. Elated, convinced that the war would soon be over, and cognisant of the unprecedented military and scientific implications, he declared: 'This is the greatest thing in history'. Some would criticise the statement as callous, but Truman was celebrating the end of a war; and, if by 'greatest', he meant 'most important', who will say he was wrong?

The *Augusta* docked at Newport News on August 7th. The next day, Truman conferred with Stimson, who showed him photographs detailing the damage at Hiroshima. After examining them thoroughly, he remarked that the destruction placed a terrible responsibility upon himself and the War Department. Stimson expressed his hope that the United States would make it as easy as possible for Japan to surrender and would treat the defeated enemy with tact and leniency. That afternoon, Truman announced to White House reporters that the USSR had declared war on Japan. With no surrender offer, no word at all, coming from Tokyo, he did not interfere with the use of the second bomb. On August 9th, at 11.00 AM, it hit Nagasaki, a tertiary target selected because of bad weather and poor observation conditions at Kokura and Nigata. The death and devastation was perhaps half that at Hiroshima; yet it was still beyond imagination.

Would the Japanese have surrendered had they been given more time to contemplate the totality of Hiroshima? Or conversely were they more impressed by the Soviet declaration of war than by the bombs? No one can say. We know they realised an event of unique horror had occurred at Hiroshima and that the United States had announced the use of an atomic bomb. We know that civilian officials wanted to surrender but that the military leaders found the prospect unbearable. Just before midnight on August 9th, the civilian-military Supreme War Council met in the presence of the emperor. After each side made its presentation, Hirohito declared emotionally and firmly, 'I swallow my own tears and give my sanction to the proposal to accept the Allied proclamation'. . . .

Truman's Vindication

Truman acted on the certainty that the longer the war lasted, the more American fatalities would occur. Some critics have suggested that he should have engaged in a grim calculus, that he should have accepted an additional 45–50,000 American deaths rather than kill many more Japanese with the bomb. But no conceivable US president in the summer of 1945 would have done that. The critics also believe that Japan, hammered by cumulative defeats, facing an unbreakable naval blockade, and shocked by Soviet intervention, would have shortly surrendered anyway. But a brute certainty remains. Japan did not muster the will to surrender until two atomic bombs had been dropped.

Most veterans of the Pacific war felt a sense of physical salvation. One of them was Army Second Lieutenant Francis Heller, a young man whose parents had fled Austria a decade earlier. Assigned to the first wave of the invasion of Honshu, Heller instead found himself wading ashore with his men on a quiet beach. 'I thought this is where I would have been killed if not for the atomic bomb', he recalls. The thought must have entered his mind many times nine years later when he helped Harry Truman write his memoirs.

Truman, the old artilleryman who had seen the horrors of the 1914–18 War close-up, understood from his own experience the hopes and fears of the Francis Hellers of the world—young combat officers dreaming of families and futures, just as he had done a generation earlier. They were the ultimate vindication of his decision.

Dropping the Atomic Bomb Was the Only Way to Force Japan's Surrender

Donald Kagan

Japan would not have surrendered during World War II if the United States had not dropped atomic bombs on Hiroshima and Nagasaki, Donald Kagan argues in the following essay. Revisionist historians such as Gar Alperovitz are wrong when they assert that Japan was already considering surrender prior to the August 1945 bombings, according to Kagan. The military leaders of Japan were prepared to continue fighting and were supported in those efforts by the Japanese government. Kagan writes that Truman could not seek anything other than the unconditional surrender of Japan and that it was the decision to drop the bombs on Japan that led to Emperor Hirohito's agreeing to surrender. Kagan is the Hillhouse Professor of history and classics at Yale University and the author of *On the Origins of War and the Preservation of Peace.*

O N AUGUST 6, 1945 THE AMERICAN WAR PLANE *ENOLA Gay* dropped an atomic bomb on Hiroshima, killing between 70,000 and 100,000 Japanese. Three days later another atomic device was exploded over Nagasaki.

Excerpted from "Why America Dropped the Bomb," by Donald Kagan, *Commentary,* September 1995. Reprinted with permission.

Within a few days Japan surrendered, and the terrible struggle that we call World War II was over.

At the time, the American people cheered the bombings without restraint, and for the simplest of reasons. As the literary historian Paul Fussell, then a combat soldier expecting to take part in the anticipated invasion of Japan, would later recall:

> We learned to our astonishment that we would not be obliged in a few months to rush up the beaches near Tokyo assault-firing while being machine-gunned, mortared, and shelled, and for all the practiced phlegm of our tough facades we broke down and cried with relief and joy. We were going to live.

At that moment, few if any Americans doubted that the purpose of this first use of atomic bombs was to bring the war to the swiftest possible end, and thereby to avert American casualties.

The Rise of the Revisionists

But the moment was short-lived. As early as 1946, challenges to the dominant opinion appeared and soon multiplied. To a large extent, the early revisionists—prominent among them such figures as Norman Cousins, P.M.S. Blackett, Carl Marzani, and the historians William Appleman Williams and D.F. Fleming—were influenced by the emerging cold war, whose origins, for the most part, they attributed to American policy under President Truman. As one exemplar of the new revisionist movement put it:

> The bomb was dropped primarily for its effect not on Japan but on the Soviet Union. One, to force a Japanese surrender before the USSR came into the Far Eastern war, and two, to show under war conditions the power of the bomb. Only in this way could a policy of intimidation [of the Soviet Union] be successful.

Another phrased the same purpose in different words:

The United States dropped the bomb to end the war against Japan and thereby stop the Russians in Asia, and to give them sober pause in Eastern Europe.

Gar Alperovitz's Argument

In 1965, in *Atomic Diplomacy: Hiroshima and Potsdam,* Gar Alperovitz picked up the main themes of the earlier writers, arguing for them now on the basis of new documentation and in a cultural climate—the climate of the mid-60's—newly hospitable to revisionist interpretations of American motives and behavior. According to Alperovitz, the bombs were not needed "to end the war and save lives—and . . . this was understood by American leaders at the time." Their aim, he wrote, was political, not military; their target was not Japan but the Soviet Union.

The chief villain was Harry Truman, who, in Alperovitz's reading, was bent on reversing Franklin D. Roosevelt's policy of peaceful accommodation with the Soviets. Thus, when he learned of the prospect of the bomb, Truman decided to delay the Allied meeting at Potsdam until the weapon could be tested. If it worked, he could take a tougher line in Eastern Europe and, perhaps, end the war before the Soviets were able to make gains in East Asia. In his eagerness to achieve these political goals, Truman failed to give proper attention to Japanese peace feelers; refused to change the demand for unconditional surrender, which was a barrier to Japanese acceptance of peace terms; and did not wait to see if Soviet entry into the Asian war might by itself cause Japan to surrender. In short, the confidence provided by the American monopoly on atomic weapons allowed Truman to launch, at Japan's expense, a "diplomatic offensive" against the Soviet Union, one which would play a role of great importance in engendering the subsequent cold war.

Because of his more detailed arguments, resting in part on newly available documents; because protest over the Vietnam war was raising questions about the origins of the cold war; and because a new generation of American diplomatic historians, trained or influenced by early revisionists like William Appleman Williams, had come onto the academic scene, Alperovitz's book enjoyed great influence and established the direction which the debate over Hiroshima has taken up to this very day. Indeed, Alperovitz is in many ways the "dean" of atomic revisionism. A second edition of his book was published in 1985, and the latest version has just appeared under the title *The Decision to Use the Atomic Bomb*; a summary version was published as an article, "Hiroshima: Historians Reassess," in the Summer 1995 issue of the quarterly *Foreign Policy*.

Alperovitz's eminence is all the more remarkable in that both his chief thesis and most of his arguments have, from their first appearance, been shredded by other scholars, his fellow revisionists among them. In, for example, *The Politics of War and United States Foreign Policy, 1943–1945* (1968), Gabriel Kolko, without mentioning Alperovitz or his book by name, directly refuted almost all his findings. Other revisionist critics found, in the words of a 1974 summary of their views, that

> the book strained the evidence, failed critically to assess sources, neglected the Roosevelt period, addressed the wrong questions, exaggerated the impact of the bomb, misunderstood Truman, and forced events into a dubious pattern.

The New Generation of Revisionists

This new generation of revisionists, notably Martin J. Sherwin and Barton J. Bernstein, stressed the essential continuity between the policies of Truman and those of Roosevelt, who had also insisted on secrecy and on keeping information about the atomic bomb away from the Soviets. Where Sherwin found no evidence of an elaborately planned showdown or "strategy of delay" in dealing with the Russians, Bernstein was even more emphatic. In his view, the hope of using the atomic bomb to produce and "cement" a peace that was to America's liking was only "a tasty bonus," and was in no way "essential to propel American leaders in 1945 to use the bomb on Japan."

These, the findings of two of the most scholarly revisionist historians, amounted to a rejection of a basic tenet of the tradition as represented by Alperovitz. And yet, even as they demolished his arguments, the new revisionists remained wedded to a number of his major conclusions. By the time these newer scholars appeared on the scene, condemnation of the bomb had become a central element in the larger revisionist project of proving the general error and evil of American policy, and for many it could not be abandoned, whatever the cost in faithfulness to the evidence. And so, even as they conceded that the bomb had not been used to advance the incipient cold-war political interests of the U.S., they shifted the central ground of argument to another question. Granting that the bomb had been used to bring the war to a swift end in order to avoid an invasion of Japan and the consequent loss of American lives, they proceeded to question whether it was either a necessary or a morally acceptable means to that end. Their answer was: no.

That, in a nutshell, is the answer that is still being given today, and where the argument has to be engaged. For the school that I have called "revisionist" now represents something more like a scholarly consensus, not to say a conventional wisdom universally parroted by educators, pundits, and the popular media. For distilled versions of this conventional wisdom, one need look no farther than the essays gathered in the "Special Report" which *Newsweek* devoted to the 50th anniversary of Hiroshima (July

24, 1995), or Murray Sayle's essay in the July 31, 1995 *New Yorker*, or the July 27, 1995 Peter Jennings special on ABC, *Hiroshima: Why the Bomb Was Dropped*. . . .

Japan Would Not Have Surrendered

[One] argument that the dropping of the bomb was unnecessary goes as follows. The Japanese had already been defeated, and it was only a brief matter of time before continued conventional bombing and shortages caused by the naval blockade would have made them see reason. They were, in fact, already sending out peace feelers in the hope of ending the war. If the Americans had been more forthcoming, willing to abandon their demand for unconditional surrender and to promise that Japan could retain its emperor, peace could have come without either an invasion or the use of the bomb.

This particular case rests in large part on a quite rational evaluation of the condition of Japan and its dismal military prospects in the spring of 1945, and on the evidence that Japanese officials were indeed discussing the possibility of a negotiated peace, using the Soviets as intermediaries. But neither of these lines of argument proves the point; nor do both of them taken together.

Even the most diehard military leaders of Japan knew perfectly well how grim their objective situation was. But this did not deter them from continuing the war, as the most reputable study of the Japanese side of the story makes clear. Although they did not expect a smashing and glorious triumph, they were confident of at least winning an operational victory "in the decisive battle for the homeland." Since any negotiated peace would be considered a surrender which would split the nation apart, Japan's militarists wanted to put it off as long as possible, and to enter negotiations only on the heels of a victory.

Some thought an American invasion could be repelled. Most hoped to inflict enough damage to make the invaders regroup. Others were even more determined; they "felt that it would be far better to die fighting in battle than to seek an ignominious survival by surrendering the nation and acknowledging defeat."

Premier Kantaro Suzuki supported the army's plan, and was content to prosecute the war with every means at his disposal—for that, after all, was "the way of the warrior and the path of the patriot." At a conference on June 8, 1945, in the presence of the emperor, the Japanese government formally affirmed its policy: "The nation would fight to the bitter end."

In spite of that, some Japanese officials did try to end the war by diplomatic negotiation before it was too late. Early efforts had been undertaken by minor military officials, who approached American OSS officers in Switzerland in April; but they were given no support from Tokyo. In July, some members of the Japanese government thought they could enlist the help of the Soviet Union in negotiating a peace that would not require a surrender or the occupation of the home islands. It is hard to understand why they thought the USSR would want to help a state it disliked and whose territory it coveted, especially when Japanese prospects were at their nadir; but such indeed was their hope.

The officials sent their proposals to Naotake Sato, the Japanese ambassador in Moscow. Their messages, and Sato's responses, were intercepted and must have influenced American plans considerably.

Sato warned his interlocutors in Tokyo that there was no chance of Soviet cooperation. An entry in the diary of Secretary of the Navy James V. Forrestal for July 15, 1945 reports "the gist of [Sato's] final message . . . Japan was thoroughly and completely defeated and . . . the only course open was quick and definite action recognizing such fact." Sato repeated this advice more than once, but the response from Tokyo was that the war must continue.

The Need for Unconditional Surrender

Revisionists and others have argued that the United States could have paved the way by dropping the demand for unconditional surrender, and especially that the U.S. should have indicated the emperor would be retained. But intercepts clearly revealed (according to Gerhard Weinberg in *A World at Arms*) that "the Japanese government would not accept the concept of unconditional surrender even if the institution of the imperial house were preserved." And then there were the intercepts of military messages, which led to the same conclusion—namely, as Edward J. Drea writes, that "the Japanese civil authorities might be considering peace, but Japan's military leaders, who American decision-makers believed had total control of the nation, were preparing for war to the knife."

The demand for unconditional surrender had in any case been asserted by Roosevelt and had become a national rallying cry. Truman could not lightly abandon it, nor is there reason to think that he wanted to. Both he and Roosevelt had clear memories of World War I and how its unsatisfactory conclusion had helped bring on World War II. In the former conflict, the Germans had not surrendered unconditionally; their land had not been occupied; they had not been made to accept the fact of their defeat in battle. Demagogues like Hitler had made use of this opportunity to claim that Germany had not lost but had been "stabbed in the back" by internal traitors like the socialists and the Jews, a technique that made it easier to rouse the Germans for a second great effort. In 1944, Roosevelt said that "practically all Germans deny the fact that they surrendered during the last war, but this time they are going to know it. And so are the Japs."

In the event, Truman did allow the Japanese to keep their emperor. Why did he not announce that intention in advance, to make surrender easier? Some members of the administration thought he should do so, but most feared that any advance concession would be taken as a sign of weakness, and encourage the Japanese bitter-enders in their hope that they could win a more favorable peace by holding out. And there were also those who were opposed to any policy that would leave the emperor in place. These, as it happens, were among the more liberal members of the administration, men like Dean Acheson and Archibald MacLeish. Their opposition was grounded in the belief that, as MacLeish put it, "the throne [was] an anachronistic, feudal institution, perfectly suited to the manipulation and use of anachronistic, feudal-minded groups within the country." It is also worth pointing out, as did the State Department's Soviet expert, Charles Bohlen, that a concession with regard to the emperor, as well as negotiations in response to the so-called peace feelers on any basis other than unconditional surrender, might well have been seen by the Soviets as a violation of commitments made at Yalta and as an effort to end the war before the Soviet Union could enter it.

What if the U.S. had issued a public warning that it had the atomic bomb, and described its fearful qualities? Or warned the Japanese of the imminent entry of the Soviet Union into the fighting? Or, best of all, combined both warnings with a promise that Japan could keep its emperor? Again, there are no grounds for believing that any or all of these steps would have made a difference to the determined military clique that was making Japan's decisions.

Even after the atomic bomb had exploded at Hiroshima on August 6, the Japanese refused to yield. An American announcement clarified the nature of the weapon that had done the damage, and warned that Japan could expect more of the same if it did not surrender. Still, the military held to its policy of resistance and insisted on a delay until a response was received to the latest Japanese approach to the Soviet Union. The answer came on August 8, when the

Soviets declared war and sent a large army against Japanese forces in Manchuria.

Why Japan Finally Surrendered

The foolishness of looking to the Soviets was now inescapably clear, but still Japan's leaders took no steps to end the fighting. The Minister of War, General Korechika Anami, went so far as to deny that Hiroshima had been struck by an atomic bomb. Others insisted that the U.S. had used its only bomb there, or that world opinion would prevent the Americans from using any others they might have. Then on August 9 the second atomic bomb fell on Nagasaki, again doing terrible damage.

The Nagasaki bomb convinced even Anami that "the Americans appear to have 100 atomic bombs . . . they could drop three per day. The next target might well be Tokyo." Even so, a meeting of the Imperial Council that night failed to achieve a consensus to accept defeat. Anami himself insisted that Japan continue to fight. If the Japanese people "went into the decisive battle in the homeland determined to display the full measure of patriotism . . . Japan would be able to avert the crisis facing her." The chief of the army general staff, Yoshijiro Umezu, expressed his confidence in the military's "ability to deal a smashing blow to the enemy," and added that in view of the sacrifices made by the many men who had gladly died for the emperor, "it would be inexcusable to surrender unconditionally." Admiral Soemu Toyoda, chief of the navy's general staff, argued that Japan could now use its full air power, heretofore held in reserve in the homeland. Like Anami, he did not guarantee victory, but asserted that "we do not believe that we will be possibly defeated."

These were the views of Japan's top military leaders after the explosion of two atomic bombs and the Soviet attack on Manchuria.

Premier Suzuki and the others who were by now favoring peace knew all this was madness. The Allies would never accept the military's conditions—restrictions on the extent of Japanese disarmament, on the occupation of Japan, and on trials of Japanese leaders for war crimes—and the continuation of warfare would be a disaster for the Japanese people. To break the deadlock he took the extraordinary step of asking the emperor to make the decision. (Normally no proposal was put to the emperor until it had achieved the unanimous approval of the Imperial Council.) At 2 a.m. on August 10, Emperor Hirohito responded to the premier's request by giving his sanction to the acceptance of the Allied terms. The Japanese reply included the proviso that the emperor be retained.

There was still disagreement within the American government on this subject. Public opinion was very hostile to the retention of the emperor, and in particular, as Gerhard Weinberg has written, "the articulate organizations of the American Left" resisted any concessions and "urged the dropping of additional atomic bombs instead." At last, the U.S. devised compromise language that accepted the imperial system by implication, while providing that the Japanese people could establish their own form of government.

Although the Japanese leaders found this acceptable, that was not the end of the matter. Opponents of peace tried to reverse the decision by a coup d'état. They might have succeeded had General Anami supported them, but he was unwilling to defy the emperor's orders. He solved his dilemma by committing suicide, and the plot failed. Had it succeeded, the war would have continued to a bloody end, with Japan under the brutal rule of a fanatical military clique. Some idea of the thinking of this faction is provided by an intercept of an August 15 message to Tokyo from the commander of Japan's army in China:

Such a disgrace as the surrender of several million troops without fighting is not paralleled in the world's military history, and it is absolutely impossible to submit to the unconditional surrender of a million picked troops in perfectly healthy shape. . . .

It was the emperor, then, who was decisive in causing Japan to surrender. What caused him to act in so remarkable a way? He was moved by the bomb—and by the Soviet declaration of war. (That declaration, scheduled for August 15, was itself hastened by the use of the bomb, and moved up to August 8.) But statements by the emperor and premier show clearly that they viewed the Soviet invasion as only another wartime setback. It was the bomb that changed the situation entirely.

The Decision to Drop the Bomb Saved American and Japanese Lives

Thomas B. Allen and Norman Polmar

President Truman made the correct decision to drop atomic bombs on Japan, because those attacks kept the war from continuing and thus saved hundreds of thousands of lives, Thomas B. Allen and Norman Polmar argue. Had the bombs not been dropped, the United States would likely have launched an amphibious assault against Japan. The authors suggest that such an attack could have led to hundreds of thousands of American casualties and the deaths of millions of Japanese soldiers and civilians, particularly if poison gas and germ warfare were used. In addition, the Japanese troops in Japan and throughout Asia would likely have fought to the death had the war continued. Allen and Polmar conclude that the United States would likely have won the war even without the atomic bomb, but by making the decision to drop the bomb, Truman saved numerous lives. Allen and Polmar are the authors of *Code-Name Downfall: The Secret Plan to Invade Japan—and Why Truman Dropped the Bomb*, the book from which this viewpoint has been excerpted.

Reprinted with permission from Simon and Schuster from *Code-Name Downfall: The Secret Plan to Invade Japan—and Why Truman Dropped the Bomb*, by Thomas B. Allen and Norman Polmar. Copyright © 1995 by Thomas B. Allen and Norman Polmar.

S OME POSTWAR HISTORIANS HAVE CHALLENGED PRESIDENT Truman's decision to use the atomic bomb to shorten the war and save American lives. They claim that the Allies could have ended the war by negotiating with the Japanese. Others contend dropping the bomb was patent racism and that atomic bombs would never have been dropped on the Germans. Still others have called the dropping of the bomb a cynical demonstration of U.S. power—making Hiroshima and Nagasaki not the last targets of World War II but rather the first targets of the Cold War.

A Way to Save Lives

In reality, anyone who closely and dispassionately examines the last weeks of the war would have to conclude that Truman was looking for ways to end the conflict honorably and at the lowest possible cost in American *and Japanese* lives. He had seen the Magic summaries that revealed the Japanese turning to the Soviet Union, not the United States, in a search not for peace but for negotiations. ["Magic" was the name given to the U.S. decipherment of Japanese diplomatic codes.] Because secrecy still shrouded the Magic decryptions for decades after the war, neither Truman nor any other U.S. decision maker could include Magic disclosures in his postwar memoirs. Indeed, not even the U.S. Strategic Bombing Survey, looking into the causes of Japan's defeat, had access to code-breaking intelligence. As for the use of the atomic bomb as an implied threat to the Soviet Union, geopolitics may have been on the minds of some of Truman's advisers, but the war and American lives were on his mind. Preparations for the massive amphibious assault on Japan were under way, and Truman went to Potsdam in July [1945] seeking assurance that Stalin would enter the war against Japan. Then Truman learned on July 16 that the atomic bomb would work, and he ordered it used. It was a weapon, and it *might* end the war without an invasion.

But as the events in Japan on the night of August 14–15 clearly show, the atomic bomb had not yet ended the war. Even with Hiroshima and Nagasaki destroyed and a "rain of ruin" threatened, many senior Japanese Army and Navy officers still wanted the Decisive Battle. Had the military coup succeeded, the war would have gone on, the Decisive Battle would have been fought, and hundreds of thousands of American and Japanese lives would have been lost.

How many lives? That is another question raised by the critics of Truman. They seize, for example, on Truman's recollection that General [George] Marshall had told him an invasion of Japan "would cost at a minimum one-quarter of a million casualties, and might cost as much as a million, on the American side alone, with an equal number of the enemy." Secretary of War [Henry] Stimson made a similar estimate in his postwar memoirs. These numbers were intentionally exaggerated, critics argue, to justify the dropping of the bomb. Searching for sources for those numbers, they cite the estimates that General [Douglas] MacArthur submitted to General Marshall for the crucial June 18 White House meeting at which President Truman approved plans for Downfall. MacArthur's figures were well below Truman's recollection of Marshall's estimates.

For whatever reason, MacArthur's figures were unrealistic. But far more important is what MacArthur's own intelligence officers discovered after the war. From interrogations of high-ranking Japanese staff officers, MacArthur's G-2 staff reported,

> The strategists at Imperial General Headquarters believed that, if they could succeed in inflicting unacceptable losses on the United States in the Kyushu operation, convince the American people of the huge sacrifices involved in an amphibious invasion of Japan, and make them aware of the determined fighting spirit of the Japanese army and civilian population, they might be

able to postpone, if not escape altogether, a crucial battle in the Kanto [Tokyo] area. In this way, they hoped to
gain time and grasp an opportunity which would lead to
the termination of hostility on more favorable terms
than those which unconditional surrender offered.

Deadly Battles in Japan

As Olympic neared, two U.S. Army agencies made independent estimates of invasion casualties. The Philadelphia
Quartermaster Depot—which procured everything from
combat boots to medals for the Army—ordered more than
370,000 Purple Hearts for award to the wounded and the
families of those killed in the final battles for Japan.

At the same time, on Luzon, the Sixth Army's medical
staff estimated that casualties from the Kyushu assault and
subsequent fighting to secure the southern half of the island would cost 394,000 Americans dead, wounded, and
missing. At Okinawa—in a battle that proffered many sim-
ilarities to the fighting on Kyushu—the Tenth Army suffered 7,613 soldiers and Marines killed and missing, and
31,807 wounded. Using that same 1:4 ratio for the Kyushu
battles, the Sixth Army could expect some 98,500 dead and
295,500 wounded.

Also using Okinawa as a model, where 4,907 U.S. Navy
men were killed aboard ships and 4,824 wounded, the
Kyushu assault in the face of heavy air and undersea
kamikaze attacks could have similarly inflicted ten times
the number of naval casualties—on the order of 49,000
Navy men killed and 48,000 injured.

Thus, a reasonable casualty estimate of the Kyushu assault—based on medical staff estimates and not influenced
by the politics of MacArthur's headquarters or Washington—could have been on the order of 147,504 dead and
343,000 wounded. While these numbers are of a different
magnitude than those developed by MacArthur's headquarters for President Truman's meeting with the Joint

A Pragmatic Decision

In the following excerpt from their book The Decision to Drop the Bomb, *Len Giovannitti and Fred Freed argue that the atomic bombs were dropped on Japan because there were no justifiable reasons not to do so.*

Was the decision to use the bomb justified?

In the end the decision was made because a decision not to use it could *not* be justified. At the most pragmatic level, if it were not used Congress and the public would ask angry questions about the expenditure of two billion dollars for a weapon that was then withheld from combat. American soldiers would die and their families would ask if they could have been saved had the weapon been used. The Japanese might surrender if they were told they could keep their Emperor, if they were sufficiently warned, if the Red Army came into the war. But then again they might not. The fire raids might finish Japan. But that would take longer and kill more Japanese. The invasion force was forming, the veterans of Guadalcanal, Tarawa, Iwo Jima and Okinawa. The invasion might never have to be launched, but who could be certain? The Soviets were threatening Europe and making demands in the Far East. The United States wanted to avoid conflict but wouldn't it be better if the war against Japan could be ended before the Soviet Union got into it? Wasn't it finally the duty of the government to use any weapon that would save American lives? The momentum for this decision had been building since the project began. The tentative date had been talked about in 1944. Without an overriding reason to reverse its thrust, neither [Henry L.] Stimson nor Truman nor any other leader could or wanted to stop it.

Len Giovannitti and Fred Freed, *The Decision to Drop the Bomb*. New York: Coward-McCann, 1965.

Chiefs of Staff, the estimates were developed by medical specialists experienced in battle, men who had to be ready with whole blood and plasma, medical personnel, and evacuation spaces on ships. Even allowing a contingency margin, the Sixth Army's estimates must be taken seriously. Kyushu would have been the bloodiest invasion in history. And it could have been surpassed by the assault of Honshu, which was planned to follow if the Japanese did not surrender by the spring of 1946.

The summons to the Decisive Battle was not just a patriotic shout. It was a strategy. But there was no Decisive Battle. Just as the atomic bomb gave Truman an alternative to invasion, it gave the Emperor an alternative way to end the war. By citing the "new and most cruel bomb," he could tell his people that they must surrender.

Had the invasion occurred, there could be no doubt that it would have launched the bloodiest battles of the war. Thousands of young American men and perhaps millions of Japanese soldiers and civilians would have died. Terror weapons—poison gas, possibly germ warfare, and perhaps crop-destroying chemicals—could have scarred the land and made the end of the war an Armageddon even worse than the devastation caused by two atomic bombs. A third atomic bomb was ready before the end of August. It probably would have been dropped on another Japanese city. And from what is now known about Marshall's thinking on the tactical use of atomic bombs, the plans for Operation Downfall would have been modified to include their use in support of the landings. The devastation of Japan could have been total.

In those final, desperate days in Tokyo, War Minister [Korechika] Anami could have stopped the surrender process and put Japan on the road toward ultimate catastrophe. There is no doubt that if Anami had let his samurai heart rule him, he could have rallied the Japanese military to his lost cause and fought on. And what of the millions of Japanese troops in Manchuria, China, Korea, Burma, and elsewhere in Asia? If their comrades in the homeland were fighting to the death, it seems likely that they would have done the same.

As memory of the war faded, the American fears of carnage on the beaches of Kyushu and Honshu were forgotten, and the focus of history turned to the decision to drop the bomb. Was it truly a decision motivated by a desire to save lives? At Oak Ridge, Tennessee, where components for the atomic bomb were produced, there was a billboard that showed American soldiers dying on a battlefield. "Whose son will die in the last minute of the war?" a headline on the billboard asked. That question drove the decision to drop the bomb.

Negotiations Would Not Have Succeeded

But what had been in 1945 an act of war against an enemy was viewed decades later as an act against humanity. And if in 1945 Truman saw the bomb as an alternative to a bloody invasion, his critics would claim there was a much more humane alternative: negotiations. It was a view, however, that ignores indelible realities. The Japanese had used negotiations in 1941 to mask the attack on Pearl Harbor. If Japanese leaders had wanted to negotiate in 1945, Foreign Minister Togo could have chosen to negotiate with the United States through a neutral nation rather than with the Soviet Union. Morever, as Magic intercepts revealed to American leaders, even that vain attempt at negotiations was tinged with treachery, through Togo's suggestion of a Japanese-Soviet military alliance.

The Potsdam Proclamation was not accepted by the Japanese. The atomic bomb dropped on Hiroshima did not produce a surrender. Not until the dropping of the second bomb on Nagasaki and the Soviet invasion of Japanese-held territory did the Big Six begin to seriously contemplate surrender. Still, they demanded unacceptable terms. The Emperor's broadcast, which finally ended the war, was not made until six days after that. And every day that surrender was delayed the death toll rose. Rebellious Army and Navy officers attacked and killed other Japanese, calling for continued resistance. Allied prisoners of war and civilian internees died throughout the vast Japanese Empire. More civilian internees died. Captured American B-29 crewmen were tortured, mutilated, and executed.

The Japanese people were permitted no thoughts of surrender. And among the military leadership in the final days of the war, death was more principled than surrender in any form. General Anami chose personal death rather than the death of his nation. So did the leaders of the mutiny he did nothing to stop. Their lives belonged to tradition, to the Emperor, to Japan. Had they been commanded to do so, the Decisive Battle would have been fought tenaciously by the Japanese on the beaches of Kyushu and possibly even Honshu. There can be little doubt that, even without the atomic bomb, the United States would have won the war—but at the cost of tens of thousands of American lives and possibly millions of Japanese lives. President Truman's decision to use the bomb ended the war and saved those lives.

Dropping the Atomic Bomb Was Unnecessary

Gar Alperovitz

Some historians have argued that Truman did not need to drop atomic bombs on Hiroshima and Nagasaki because World War II was already nearing an end and Japan would have soon surrendered. One such historian is Gar Alperovitz, who in the following 1990 essay writes that Truman and U.S. military leaders were aware in spring 1945 that Japan was seeking to end the war and would surrender to the United States, as long as Emperor Hirohito was not removed from power. In addition, Alperovitz writes that even if Japan had not surrendered in spring 1945, it would have once the Soviet Union declared war against Japan. He notes that it was that declaration of war, which took place just two days after the Hiroshima bombing, which led to the surrender. Alperovitz is the president of the National Center for Economic and Security Alternatives, a politically progressive research institute, and the author of *Atomic Diplomacy: Hiroshima and Potsdam*.

A SK THE AVERAGE PERSON WHY THE UNITED STATES EX-ploded the atomic bomb over Hiroshima and Nagasaki [in August 1945] and the answer will almost always be straightforward: "To save thousands of lives by making an invasion unnecessary at the end of World War II." ABC's Ted Koppel expressed such a view in a special "Nightline"

Excerpted from "Why America Dropped the Bomb," by Gar Alperovitz, *Technology Review*, August/September 1990. Reprinted by permission of *Technology Review* via the Copyright Clearance Center.

broadcast [in the 1980s]: "What happened over Japan . . . was a human tragedy. . . . But what was planned to take place in the war between Japan and the United States would almost certainly have been an even greater tragedy."

The Atomic Bomb Was Not the Only Solution

The only problem with this morally comforting explanation is that it is now known to be false. Consider this statement: "The consensus among scholars is that the bomb was not needed to avoid an invasion of Japan. . . . It is clear that alternatives to the bomb existed and that Truman and his advisers knew it." The writer is not a radical revisionist but rather J. Samuel Walker, chief historian of the U.S. Nuclear Regulatory Commission. Nor is this a personal opinion: Walker is summing up the weight of modern historical studies in the respected journal *Diplomatic History*.

Scholarly judgment has shifted with the discovery of a wide range of previously unavailable documents, diaries, and private journals. In particular, as University of Illinois historian Robert Messer has written, the personal diaries of President Harry Truman have been "devastating" to the traditional argument that detonating the bomb was the only way to avoid a U.S. invasion.

The conclusions of Walker and Messer echo the judgment of the official U.S. Strategic Bombing Survey, which assessed the issue in 1946: "Certainly prior to 31 December 1945, and in all probability prior to 1 November 1945, Japan would have surrendered even if the atomic bombs had not been dropped, even if Russia had not entered the war, and even if no invasion had been planned or contemplated."

The bare chronology of events in 1945 itself raises questions about U.S. motives for dropping the bomb. Germany surrendered on May 8, and the Allied powers knew that Japan's situation was deteriorating rapidly. At the Yalta conference of Allied leaders in February, Stalin had agreed to declare war on Japan three months after the defeat of

Germany—roughly August 8. The United States originally sought Soviet support for an invasion of Japan, but by late summer the shock of a Russian declaration of war seemed likely to end the war without a U.S. offensive.

The *Enola Gay* dropped its world-shattering cargo over Hiroshima on August 6. On August 8, the Soviet Union informed Japan it was entering the war. The second atomic weapon exploded over Nagasaki on August 9. The first U.S. landing on Japan was still another three months off, and a full invasion was not expected to take place—even on paper—until the spring of 1946.

Nobel Prize–winning British physicist P.M.S. Blackett pointed out as long ago as 1948 how this sequence challenged the official rationale for the bombings. Was it really the case—with three months still to go before a U.S. landing—that American and British leaders saw no alternative except detonating the bomb? . . .

Japan Seeks a Way Out

President Truman's oft-quoted estimate that a U.S. invasion might have cost a million American lives is the basis for much of the conventional wisdom about why the bomb was dropped. Unfortunately, that figure has no basis in military planning records. Stanford historian Barton Bernstein has shown that the Joint War Plans Committee—a high-level advisory group to the U.S. Joint Chiefs of Staff—concluded that about 40,000 Americans would die if an assault were launched on both the island of Kyushu and, thereafter, the main Japanese home island.

But as early as mid-June 1945—and even without a Soviet attack—it appeared that the smaller Kyushu landing alone might "well prove to be the decisive operation which will terminate the war," according to the committee. U.S. Army Chief of Staff General George C. Marshall informed President Truman that casualties for the Kyushu operation were not expected to exceed 31,000 during the first and costliest month of the operation—a figure that included dead, wounded, and missing. Extrapolating from contemporary combat statistics would yield an estimate of less than 7,500 dead.

However, these deaths would occur only if such a landing were actually attempted, and by mid-summer 1945 that possibility had become "remote," in the judgment of a newly discovered intelligence study. Massive documentation now shows that Japan's military, economic, and political condition deteriorated dramatically from the spring of 1945 on. Even as early as April 1945, General Douglas MacArthur, commander of U.S. troops in the Pacific, reported that "the Japanese fleet has been reduced to practical impotency. The Japanese Air Force has been reduced to a line of action which involves uncoordinated, suicidal attacks against our forces. . . . Its attrition is heavy and its power for sustained action is diminishing rapidly."

As the situation in Japan worsened, Japanese "peace feelers" began to erupt throughout Europe. On May 12, 1945, Office of Strategic Services Director William Donovan reported to President Truman that Shunichi Kase, Japan's minister to Switzerland, wished "to help arrange for a cessation of hostilities." He believed "one of the few provisions the Japanese would insist upon would be the retention of the Emperor."

Truman received a similar report concerning Masutaro Inoue, Japan's counselor in Portugal, who, according to an Office of Strategic Services informant, "declared that actual peace terms were unimportant so long as the term 'unconditional surrender' was not employed. The Japanese, he asserted, are convinced that within a few weeks all of their wood and paper houses will be destroyed."

Though such feelers were not yet official, in mid-June Admiral William D. Leahy—who both chaired the Joint Chiefs of Staff and served as the president's chief of staff—concluded that "a surrender of Japan can be arranged with terms that can be accepted by Japan and that will make fully satisfactory provision for America's defense against future trans-Pacific aggression."

The United States Knew Japan's Intentions

Even more important evidence of Japan's desire to end hostilities reached the White House through intercepted diplomatic cables. U.S. intelligence experts had broken Japanese codes early in the war. During the late summer, these experts learned that the emperor of Japan was secretly attempting to arrange a surrender through Russia. The emperor wished to send a personal representative, Prince Konoye, to Moscow: "The mission . . . was to ask the Soviet Government to take part in mediation to end the present war and to transmit the complete Japanese case in this respect. . . . Prince Konoe [sic] was especially charged by His Majesty, the Emperor, to convey to the Soviet Government that it was exclusively the desire of His Majesty to avoid more bloodshed."

Initial approaches to Russia can be traced as far back as 1944. The emperor's personal initiative, however, was "real evidence," as Secretary of the Navy James Forrestal put it, of a determination to end the fighting. The intercepted cables also indicated that the only significant condition appeared to be an assurance that the emperor could retain his title.

Truman later acknowledged that he had generally been informed of these messages, but his personal, handwritten journal—kept secret and, so we are told, then misfiled until 1979—is particularly revealing. In it he goes so far as to characterize one crucial Japanese intercept as the "telegram from [the] Jap Emperor asking for peace."

As these cables made clear, and as several top officials advised the president, one option that appeared likely to end the war was simply to let Japan know that "unconditional surrender" did not require removing the emperor. Indeed, since the Japanese people considered the emperor a deity, U.S. and British intelligence experts argued that without such assurances, Japan would be forced to fight to save face until the very end. U.S. military leaders also believed that only if the emperor were allowed to keep his throne would anyone have enough authority to order Japanese soldiers to put down their arms.

It is important to understand that a variety of documents, including the diaries of Secretary of War Henry L. Stimson and the papers of Acting Secretary of State Joseph C. Grew, show that President Truman had no fundamental objection to offering assurances to the emperor: he made this quite clear to both men at different points during the summer. And, of course, Truman ultimately did allow the emperor to remain: Japan has an emperor to this day.

The president chose to wait, however, until after using the atomic bomb before providing the assurances Japan sought. One common interpretation is that he feared domestic political opponents would criticize him for being "soft" on the Japanese. He may have hoped the bomb would make even small changes in the surrender terms unnecessary. But by July 1945 the choice was clearly no longer the simple one of mounting an invasion or relying on the devastating power of the new weapon.

The Role of the Soviets

Not only was Japan known to be on the verge of surrender, but an attack by the massive Red Army would clearly be disastrous, especially since Germany's capitulation had left Japan isolated. Indeed, the position of the "war party" within the Japanese Cabinet rested heavily on keeping the Soviet Union neutral.

This is an area where new evidence is particularly important. Prime Minister [Winston] Churchill argued as early as September 1944 that even a public statement that Russia was about to enter the war would have enormous impact: "From all I have learnt about the internal state of

Japan and the sense of hopelessness weighing on their people, I believe it might well be that once the Nazis are shattered a triple summons to Japan to surrender, coming from our three Great Powers, might be decisive."

Repeated U.S. intelligence studies also judged as early as mid-April 1945 that "the entry of the U.S.S.R. into the war would . . . convince most Japanese at once of the inevitability of complete defeat." In mid-June 1945, General Marshall advised President Truman directly that the impact of the expected Soviet declaration of war "on the already hopeless Japanese" might well "lever" them into capitulation immediately or shortly thereafter "if" the United States landed in Japan. A month later—with still more information in hand—Britain's General Sir Hastings Ismay summarized joint American-British intelligence conclusions for Prime Minister Churchill, saying: "[W]hen Russia came into the war against Japan, the Japanese would probably wish to get out on almost any terms short of the dethronement of the Emperor."

Truman's private journal, along with his letters, also illuminates his recognition, well before the atomic bomb was used, that the Soviet declaration of war—on its own—seemed all but certain to end the fighting. After Stalin confirmed that Russia would declare war against Japan in early August, Truman privately noted: "Fini Japs when that comes about." And writing to his wife, the president observed that with the Soviet declaration, "We'll end the war a year sooner now, and think of the kids who won't be killed!" (Military planners advised that if an invasion were undertaken, the war's likely maximum duration would be about a year.) So important did the Russian declaration seem before the first atomic test that Truman told several people it was his main reason for traveling to Potsdam, Germany, to meet with Stalin in July.

Since the U.S. bombings of Japan and the Soviet declaration of war occurred within days of each other, and since

Japan formally surrendered only after Truman acknowledged the role of the emperor, historians continue to debate precisely how much weight to accord each factor in ending the conflict. But a top-secret 1946 War Department intelligence study discovered [in 1989] bluntly concludes that the atomic bomb had little to do with Japan's decision to surrender. Rather, it states that the Soviet Union's entry was unquestionably the decisive factor that ended World War II. Like the official Strategic Bombing Survey, the study also concludes that a large-scale U.S. invasion would likely never have taken place: it is "almost a certainty that the Japanese would have capitulated upon the entry of Russia into the war."

Protests Against the Bomb

Despite the accumulating evidence that Japan was all but defeated, plans to ready the bomb continued throughout the spring of 1945. However, as Japan's situation worsened during May, June, and July, the specific role the bomb was to play appears to have shifted. Initially some U.S. leaders felt the weapon should be employed in the course of an invasion against strictly military targets. Even as [late as] May 29, General Marshall thought "these weapons might first be used against straight military objectives such as a large naval installation and then if no complete result was derived from the effect of that, . . . we ought to designate a number of large manufacturing areas from which people would be warned to leave—telling the Japanese that we intend to destroy such centers."

By early June, however, Japan's condition had so deteriorated that a psychological shock—not an attack to destroy "straight military objectives"—seemed likely to produce surrender. But the Interim Committee, a high-level group formed to decide how to handle the new technology and chaired by Secretary of War Henry L. Stimson, rejected the option of giving an explicit warning to civilians.

The Bombs Did Not Defeat Japan

The Strategic Bombing Survey was a group of experts who issued a report in 1946 on the impact of the atomic bombs on Japan. In the following excerpt from that report, the survey contends that while the bombs may have shortened the war, they did not cause Japan's surrender.

The Hiroshima and Nagasaki atomic bombs did not defeat Japan, nor by the testimony of the enemy leaders who ended the war did they persuade Japan to accept unconditional surrender. The Emperor, the Lord Privy Seal, the Prime Minister, the Foreign Minister, and the Navy Minister had decided as early as May of 1945 that the war should be ended even if it meant acceptance of defeat on allied terms. The War Minister and the two chiefs of staff opposed unconditional surrender. The impact of the Hiroshima attack was to bring further urgency and lubrication to the machinery of achieving peace, primarily by contributing to a situation which permitted the Prime Minister to bring the Emperor overtly and directly into a position where his decision for immediate acceptance of the Potsdam Declaration could be used to override the remaining objectors. Thus, although the atomic bombs changed no votes of the Supreme War Direction Council concerning the Potsdam terms, they did foreshorten the war and expedite the peace.

"Strategic Bombing Survey," excerpted in Barton J. Bernstein and Allen J. Matusow, eds., *The Truman Administration: A Documentary History*. New York: Harper & Row, 1966.

According to the committee's records, "The Secretary expressed the conclusion, on which there was general agreement, that . . . we should seek to make a profound psychological impression on as many of the inhabitants as possible. At the suggestion of Dr. Conant [the president of Harvard] the Secretary agreed that the most desirable target would be a vital war plant employing a large number of workers and closely surrounded by workers' houses." And the conservative historian Paul Johnson bitterly comments in his *Modern Times,* "When the time came to determine the first target for the atomic bomb, it was the President of Harvard, James Conant representing the interests of civilization . . . , who made the decisive suggestion."

Various scientists, upset that the bombing would proceed even though Germany had been defeated and Japan had been reduced to dire straits, attempted to head it off. New research has also given us a clearer picture of the many ways their efforts were blocked. Peter Wyden, for instance, describes in his *Day One* how J. Robert Oppenheimer deftly sidetracked Chicago scientists opposed to using the atomic weapon. General Leslie Groves, the military leader of the Manhattan Project, and other top officials also simply delayed a petition to the president registering scientists' opposition until it was too late.

Wesleyan political scientist Leon V. Sigal has shown how the dissident scientists' challenges prompted a change in the fundamental role and composition of the Interim Committee. Its initial task was to plan for post-war handling of atomic weapons and atomic energy. But, Sigal suggests, "Consideration by the committee . . . of how to use the bomb against Japan was part of a bureaucratic strategy of senior War Department [and other] officials with organization interests in dropping the bomb on Japan's cities." He concludes that "the committee was . . . a blocking maneuver to blunt the dissidents by preventing their options and arguments from reaching President Truman and by getting other scientists to endorse the option already chosen by the Target Committee."

Several high-level military leaders, when told of the decision to drop the bomb, were deeply offended. General

Dwight D. Eisenhower, commander of U.S. forces in Europe, reported this reaction after Secretary of War Henry L. Stimson informed him in mid-July of the plan: "During his recitation of the relevant facts, I had been conscious of a feeling of depression and so I voiced to him my grave misgivings, first on the basis of my belief that Japan was already defeated and that dropping the bomb was completely unnecessary, and secondly because I thought that our country should avoid shocking world opinion by the use of a weapon whose employment was, I thought, no longer mandatory as a measure to save American lives." Eisenhower's assessment was blunt: "Japan was at that very moment seeking some way to surrender with a minimum loss of 'face'. . . . It wasn't necessary to hit them with that awful thing."

Similarly, the reaction of Britain's General [Lionel Hastings] Ismay to attacking Japanese cities with the new weapon was "revulsion." He added, "For some time past it had been firmly fixed in my mind that the Japanese were tottering." And Admiral Leahy, the highest U.S. military official, minced few words in recounting his view of this period. The "Japanese were already defeated and ready to surrender. . . . The use of this barbarous weapon against Hiroshima and Nagasaki was of no material assistance in our war against Japan. . . . [I]n being the first to use it, we . . . adopted an ethical standard common to the barbarians of the Dark Ages. I was not taught to make war in that fashion, and wars cannot be won by destroying women and children." . . .

Waiting for the Full Truth

The full record of what happened in the summer of 1945 is still not available. We especially lack knowledge of many private discussions between Secretary Byrnes and President Truman during April, May, and June 1945, when Byrnes served as the president's personal representative on the Interim Committee. We know almost nothing about the critical planning sessions the two men held during the eight-day Atlantic crossing before the Potsdam conference and the bombing itself. Beyond this, many official documents—ranging from selected Japanese "intercepts" to specific Manhattan Project files—are still classified, and some private journals have not been made public.

We shall undoubtedly learn the full truth one day. As the Cold War winds down, there is renewed interest in the Hiroshima story—and in the profound questions Secretary Stimson and others came to understand were posed by the first use of nuclear weapons, and by the U.S. contribution to the tensions that were to dominate international relations for more than four decades.

Truman Failed as a Statesman When He Decided to Drop the Bomb

John Rawls

Political philosopher John Rawls argues that President Truman acted immorally when he chose to end World War II by dropping atomic bombs. Rawls believes the decision was a great evil because it was contrary to the ways in which a democratic nation should conduct itself during war. Specifically, civilians should not be attacked except in cases of extreme crisis, a situation that Rawls argues did not apply to the United States in its war against Japan. Writing in 1995, Rawls also suggests that Truman was a poor statesman because the president failed to enter into negotiations with Japan prior to the bombings. Rawls is a professor at Harvard University.

T HE FIFTIETH YEAR SINCE THE BOMBING OF HIROSHIMA IS a time to reflect about what one should think of it. Is it really a great wrong, as many now think, and many also thought then, or is it perhaps justified after all? I believe that both the fire-bombing of Japanese cities beginning in the spring of 1945 and the later atomic bombing of Hi-

Excerpted from "Fifty Years After Hiroshima," by John Rawls, *Dissent*, Summer 1995. Reprinted with permission. The author's endnotes in the original have been omitted in this reprint.

roshima on August 6 were very great wrongs, and rightly seen as such. In order to support this opinion, I set out what I think to be the principles governing the conduct of war—*jus in bello*—of democratic peoples. These peoples have different ends of war than nondemocratic, especially totalitarian, states, such as Germany and Japan, which sought the domination and exploitation of subjected peoples, and in Germany's case, their enslavement if not extermination.

Six Principles of War

Although I cannot properly justify them here, I begin by setting out six principles and assumptions in support of these judgments. I hope they seem not unreasonable; and certainly they are familiar, as they are closely related to much traditional thought on this subject.

1. The aim of a just war waged by a decent democratic society is a just and lasting peace between peoples, especially with its present enemy.

2. A decent democratic society is fighting against a state that is not democratic. This follows from the fact that democratic peoples do not wage war against each other; and since we are concerned with the rules of war as they apply to such peoples, we assume the society fought against is nondemocratic and that its expansionist aims threatened the security and free institutions of democratic regimes and caused the war.

3. In the conduct of war, a democratic society must carefully distinguish three groups: the state's leaders and officials, its soldiers, and its civilian population. The reason for these distinctions rests on the principle of responsibility: since the state fought against is not democratic, the civilian members of the society cannot be those who organized and brought on the war. This was done by its leaders and officials assisted by other elites who control and staff the state apparatus. They are responsible, they willed the

war, and for doing that, they are criminals. But civilians, often kept in ignorance and swayed by state propaganda, are not. And this is so even if some civilians knew better and were enthusiastic for the war. In a nation's conduct of war many such marginal cases may exist, but they are irrelevant. As for soldiers, they, just as civilians, and leaving aside the upper ranks of an officer class, are not responsible for the war, but are conscripted or in other ways forced into it, their patriotism often cruelly and cynically exploited. The grounds on which they may be attacked directly are not that they are responsible for the war but that a democratic people cannot defend itself in any other way, and defend itself it must do. About this there is no choice.

4. A decent democratic society must respect the human rights of the members of the other side, both civilians and soldiers. . . . This means, as I understand it here, that they can never be attacked directly except in times of extreme crisis, the nature of which I discuss below.

5. Continuing with the thought of teaching the content of human rights, the next principle is that just peoples by their actions and proclamations are to foreshadow during war the kind of peace they aim for and the kind of relations they seek between nations. By doing so, they show in an open and public way the nature of their aims and the kind of people they are. These last duties fall largely on the leaders and officials of the governments of democratic peoples, since they are in the best position to speak for the whole people and to act as the principle applies. Although all the preceding principles also specify duties of statesmanship, this is especially true of 4 and 5. The way a war is fought and the actions ending it endure in the historical memory of peoples and may set the stage for future war. This duty of statesmanship must always be held in view.

6. Finally, we note the place of practical means-end reasoning in judging the appropriateness of an action or policy for achieving the aim of war or for not causing more

harm than good. This mode of thought—whether carried on by (classical) utilitarian reasoning, or by cost-benefit analysis, or by weighing national interests, or in other ways—must always be framed within and strictly limited by the preceding principles. The norms of the conduct of war set up certain lines that bound just action. War plans and strategies, and the conduct of battles, must lie within their limits. (The only exception, I repeat, is in times of extreme crisis.)

Defining the Statesman

In connection with the fourth and fifth principles of the conduct of war, I have said that they are binding especially on the leaders of nations. They are in the most effective position to represent their people's aims and obligations, and sometimes they become statesmen. But who is a statesman? There is no office of statesman, as there is of president, or chancellor, or prime minister. The statesman is an ideal, like the ideal of the truthful or virtuous individual. Statesmen are presidents or prime ministers who become statesmen through their exemplary performance and leadership in their office in difficult and trying times and manifest strength, wisdom, and courage. They guide their people through turbulent and dangerous periods for which they are esteemed always, as one of their great statesmen.

The ideal of the statesman is suggested by the saying: the politician looks to the next election, the statesman to the next generation. It is the task of the student of philosophy to look to the permanent conditions and the real interests of a just and good democratic society. It is the task of the statesman, however, to discern these conditions and interests in practice; the statesman sees deeper and further than most others and grasps what needs to be done. The statesman must get it right, or nearly so, and hold fast to it. Washington and Lincoln were statesmen. [Chancellor Otto von] Bismarck was not. He did not see Germany's real interests far enough into the future and his judgment and motives were often distorted by his class interests and his wanting himself alone to be chancellor of Germany. Statesmen need not be selfless and may have their own interests when they hold office, yet they must be selfless in their judgments and assessments of society's interests and not be swayed, especially in war and crisis, by passions of revenge and retaliation against the enemy.

Above all, they are to hold fast to the aim of gaining a just peace, and avoid the things that make achieving such a peace more difficult. Here the proclamations of a nation should make clear (the statesman must see to this) that the enemy people are to be granted an autonomous regime of their own and a decent and full life once peace is securely reestablished. Whatever they may be told by their leaders, whatever reprisals they may reasonably fear, they are not to be held as slaves or serfs after surrender, or denied in due course their full liberties; and they may well achieve freedoms they did not enjoy before, as the Germans and the Japanese eventually did. The statesman knows, if others do not, that all descriptions of the enemy people (not their rulers) inconsistent with this are impulsive and false.

America Was Not Facing a Crisis

Turning now to Hiroshima and the fire-bombing of Tokyo, we find that neither falls under the exemption of extreme crisis. One aspect of this is that since (let's suppose) there are no absolute rights—rights that must be respected in all circumstances—there are occasions when civilians can be attacked directly by aerial bombing. Were there times during the war when Britain could properly have bombed Hamburg and Berlin? Yes, when Britain was alone and desperately facing Germany's superior might; moreover, this period would extend until Russia had clearly beat off the first German assault in the summer and fall of 1941, and would be able to fight Germany until the end. . . .

Yet it is clear that while the extreme crisis exemption held for Britain in the early stages of the war, it never held at any time for the United States in its war with Japan. The principles of the conduct of war were always applicable to it. Indeed, in the case of Hiroshima many involved in higher reaches of the government recognized the questionable character of the bombing and that limits were being crossed. Yet during the discussions among allied leaders in June and July 1945, the weight of the practical means-end reasoning carried the day. Under the continuing pressure of war, such moral doubts as there were failed to gain an express and articulated view. As the war progressed, the heavy fire-bombing of civilians in the capitals of Berlin and Tokyo and elsewhere was increasingly accepted on the allied side. Although after the outbreak of war Roosevelt had urged both sides not to commit the inhuman barbarism of bombing civilians, by 1945 allied leaders came to assume that Roosevelt would have used the bomb on Hiroshima. The bombing grew out of what had happened before.

An Evil Decision

The practical means-end reasons to justify using the atomic bomb on Hiroshima were the following:

The bomb was dropped to hasten the end of the war. It is clear that Truman and most other allied leaders thought it would do that. Another reason was that it would save lives where the lives counted are the lives of American soldiers. The lives of Japanese, military or civilian, presumably counted for less. Here the calculations of least time and most lives saved were mutually supporting. Moreover, dropping the bomb would give the Emperor and the Japanese leaders a way to save face, an important matter given Japanese samurai culture. Indeed, at the end a few top Japanese leaders wanted to make a last sacrificial stand but were overruled by others supported by the Emperor, who ordered surrender on August 12, having received

The crew of the B-29 bomber that dropped the bomb on Nagasaki.

word from Washington that the Emperor could stay provided it was understood that he had to comply with the orders of the American military commander. The last reason I mention is that the bomb was dropped to impress the Russians with American power and make them more agreeable with our demands. This reason is highly disputed but urged by some critics and scholars as important.

The failure of these reasons to reflect the limits on the conduct of war is evident, so I focus on a different matter: the failure of statesmanship on the part of allied leaders and why it might have occurred. Truman once described the Japanese as beasts and to be treated as such; yet how foolish it sounds now to call the Germans or the Japanese barbarians and beasts! Of the Nazis and Tojo militarists, yes, but they are not the German and the Japanese people. Churchill later granted that he carried the bombing too far, led by passion and the intensity of the conflict. A duty of statesmanship is not to allow such feelings, natural and inevitable as they may be, to alter the course a democratic people should best follow in striving for peace. The statesman understands that relations with the present enemy have special importance: for as I have said, war must be openly and publicly conducted in ways that make a lasting and amicable peace possible with a defeated enemy, and prepares its people for how they may be expected to be treated. Their present fears of being subjected to acts of revenge and retaliation must be put to rest; present enemies must be seen as associates in a shared and just future peace.

These remarks make it clear that, in my judgment, both Hiroshima and the fire-bombing of Japanese cities were great evils that the duties of statesmanship require political leaders to avoid in the absence of the crisis exemption. I also believe this could have been done at little cost in further casualties. An invasion was unnecessary at that date, as the war was effectively over. However, whether that is true or not makes no difference. Without the crisis exemption, those bombings are great evils. Yet it is clear that an articulate expression of the principles of just war introduced at that time would not have altered the outcome. It was simply too late. A president or prime minister must have carefully considered these questions, preferably long before, or at least when they had the time and leisure to think things out. Reflections on just war cannot be heard in the daily round of the pressure of events near the end of the hostilities; too many are anxious and impatient, and simply worn out. . . .

Another failure of statesmanship was not to try to enter negotiations with the Japanese before any drastic steps such as the fire-bombing of cities or the bombing of Hiroshima were taken. A conscientious attempt to do so was morally necessary. As a democratic people, we owed that to the Japanese people—whether to their government is another matter. There had been discussions in Japan for some time about finding a way to end the war, and on June 26 the government had been instructed by the Emperor to do so. It must surely have realized that with the navy destroyed and the outer islands taken, the war was lost. True, the Japanese were deluded by the hope that the Russians might prove to be their allies, but negotiations are precisely to disabuse the other side of delusions of that kind. A statesman is not free to consider that such negotiations may lessen the desired shock value of subsequent attacks.

Truman's Failure

Truman was in many ways a good, at times a very good president. But the way he ended the war showed he failed as a statesman. For him it was an opportunity missed, and a loss to the country and its armed forces as well. It is sometimes said that questioning the bombing of Hiroshima is an insult to the American troops who fought the war. This is hard to understand. We should be able to look back and consider our faults after fifty years. We expect the Germans and the Japanese to do that—"*Vergangenheitsverarbeitung*"—as the Germans say. Why shouldn't we? It can't be that we think we waged the war without moral error! . . .

CHAPTER
2

THE TRUMAN DOCTRINE AND THE REBUILDING OF EUROPE

The Truman Doctrine Increased Truman's Authority

Lynn Boyd Hinds and Theodore Otto Windt Jr.

In February 1947, the British government announced that it could no longer afford to provide military and economic aid to Greece and Turkey, two nations that were then struggling against communist forces. One month later, President Truman told Congress his plan to help the two nations and contain communism in Europe; that plan would become known as the Truman Doctrine. In the following selection, Lynn Boyd Hinds and Theodore Otto Windt Jr. write that Truman authored a significant change in American foreign policy that also succeeded in strengthening his authority as a world leader. According to the authors, the Truman Doctrine was a historic decision that united Americans against communism. Hinds is a professor of communication at Drury College in Springfield, Missouri, and Windt is a professor of communication at the University of Pittsburgh.

O N MARCH 12, 1947 PRESIDENT TRUMAN ADDRESSED A special joint session of Congress. His speech was a rambling address reflecting the many people who had a hand in its construction. The speech has been so thoroughly analyzed by so many scholars that a detailed analysis of it would be redundant. Our purpose here will be to

Excerpted from *The Cold War as Rhetoric: The Beginnings, 1945-1950*, by Lynn Boyd Hinds and Theodore Otto Windt Jr. Copyright © 1991 by Lynn Boyd Hinds and Theodore Otto Windt Jr. Reproduced with permission of Greenwood Publishing Group, Inc., Westport, CT.

summarize the speech and point to the parts that played the major role in developing the anticommunism consensus. Despite the brevity of his remarks and the plain style he employed, Truman had the electrifying effect he sought.

Greece and Turkey as Symbols

In the preamble of his address, President Truman stressed the gravity of the recent events. He stated that these events involved the foreign policy and national security of the United States, a world situation he subsequently called a "crisis" and one that required "immediate action." The most pressing problem, "one aspect of the present situation," involved Greece and Turkey. Thus, right off the bat, Truman implied that Greece and Turkey were only symbolic of a far more fundamental problem confronting the United States, but also that each were inextricably part of U.S. national security.

Truman announced that Greece had issued an urgent appeal for aid from the United States and briefly described the economic problems that government faced. But the problem was even greater than these financial difficulties: "The very existence of the Greek state is today threatened by the terrorist activities of several thousand armed men, led by Communists, who defy the government's authority at a number of points, particularly along the northern boundaries." The Greek government, Truman stated, could not cope with these problems and only the United States was in a position to render aid. After further describing the plight of the Greeks and adding disclaimers about the character of its government, Truman briefly said that Turkey too needed additional aid from both the United States and Great Britain to maintain "its national integrity."

Neither Greece nor Turkey was the main issue in this crisis. Their problems were real, according to Truman, but they were primarily symbolic of larger issues. He reminded his listeners of the "real" meaning of World War II, that the United States had fought that war to keep some nations from imposing their way of life on others. This analogy linked the recent war to the present situation and set the stage for fundamental meaning to be placed on the current crisis. Declaring that he was "fully aware of the broad implications" of the policy he was to announce, Truman launched into the meat of his speech:

> At the present moment in world history nearly every nation must choose between alternative ways of life. The choice is too often not a free one.
>
> One way of life is based upon the will of the majority, and is distinguished by free institutions, representative government, free elections, guarantees of individual liberty, freedom of speech and religion, and freedom from political oppression.
>
> The second way of life is based upon the will of a minority forcibly imposed upon the majority. It relies upon terror and oppression, a controlled press and radio, fixed elections, and the suppression of personal freedoms.
>
> I believe it must be the policy of the United States to support free peoples who are resisting attempted subjugation by armed minorities or by outside pressures.
>
> I believe that we must assist free peoples to work out their own destinies in their own way.
>
> I believe that our help should be primarily through economic and financial aid which is essential to economic stability and orderly political processes.

A New and Necessary Foreign Policy

Here was the new foreign policy for the United States and the justification for it pristinely and plainly stated. Truman declared in no uncertain terms the broad policy that would guide the country for decades. He had created the linguistic lens through which every American could see the central meaning of complex and difficult problems confronting the country in international affairs.

It should be noted that President Truman stated with equally unmistakable language that American help should "primarily" be offered through economic and financial assistance. However, by focusing almost exclusively on Greece, the country involved in a real civil war, and by describing the universal problem as one of "armed minorities" attempting to "forcibly" subjugate "freedom-loving peoples," the military images and implications overshadowed the precise call for economic aid to threatened countries. Later, when Secretary George Marshall recommended aid to European countries in his speech at Harvard, some interpreted Marshall's economic plan as an alternative to Truman's belligerence. Even more to the point, Truman did not (and probably could not at the time) say what additional measures the United States would take if economic aid did not achieve the effect he desired. It became simple for the president and others then to advocate military aid as the next step in confronting communism.

As Truman viewed the world situation, there were only two choices and the question was: Which side are you on? His vision was that of an ideological dialectic with no synthesis in sight. The president had made his choice. He contended that failure to act at this critical moment in world history would have tragic consequences. Echoing [Undersecretary of State Dean] Acheson's private presentation thirteen days earlier and presenting what would eventually be known as the "domino" theory, President Truman stated:

> If Greece should fall under the control of an armed minority, the effect upon its neighbor, Turkey, would be immediate and serious. Confusion and disorder might

well spread throughout the entire Middle East.

Moreover, the disappearance of Greece as an independent state would have a profound effect upon those countries in Europe whose peoples are struggling against great difficulties to maintain their freedoms and their independence while they repair the damages of war.

It would be an unspeakable tragedy if these countries, which have struggled so long against overwhelming odds, should lose that victory for which they sacrificed so much. Collapse of free institutions and loss of independence would be disastrous not only for them but for the world. Discouragement and possibly failure would quickly be the lot of neighboring peoples striving to maintain their freedom and independence.

Should we fail to aid Greece and Turkey in this fateful hour, the effect will be far reaching to the West as well as to the East.

Good vs. Evil

Thus did President Truman describe the stakes in the problem and the policy he was presenting to Congress and the American people. He spent the remainder of his address detailing the legislation he sought and the amount of money needed. Though the principle Truman had stated was global in scope, the money he asked for ($400 million) was minimal in aid.

In eighteen minutes President Truman had announced a significant departure in America's traditional foreign policy and had created a new way of seeing its place in the postwar world. He had created a simple good-evil perceptual lens through which the American people could view, understand, interpret, and act upon events that the administration said symbolized confrontations between two mutually exclusive "ways of life." Differences within the so-called free world and within the so-called communist world were minimized or ignored, as the moral and mortal conflict between the two was accentuated. About such language as this, Alexis de Tocqueville had observed: "Democratic writers are perpetually coining abstract words . . . in which they sublimate into further abstraction the abstract terms of the language. Moreover, to render their mode of speech more succinct, they personify the object of these abstract terms and make it act like a real person." The personifications would come later. For the moment, the abstract definition of the enemy and the abstract principle would suffice. As one Briton said: "We went to sleep in one world and woke up . . . in another.". . .

The Doctrine Boosted Truman's Authority

The authority with which one speaks directly influences belief. Part of Churchill's authority came from his person. His reputation as spokesman for freedom during World War II required that others weigh his words seriously, even if they rejected them at the time. Harry Truman's authority came from his office. He was president of the United States and he was proposing a sharp departure from traditional U.S. foreign policy. Unlike Churchill, he was in a position to implement that policy. But in this particular case, the speech lent authority to Truman.

Ever since he had been propelled into the presidency, he had been hounded by questions, mainly privately spoken but sometimes voiced in public, about whether he was up to the job. He pondered the same questions himself. With the decisive language and bold policy of this speech, he began to be transformed. Again, this was no overnight or magical transformation. His appointment of General Marshall, probably the most esteemed American citizen of the time, as secretary of state in January 1947 enhanced his authority. The other appointments early that year conveyed the image that government by crony was being replaced with government by capability. Secretary Marshall's pointed deference to the president, especially noted in his announcement about the Greek request for aid, added further to recognition of Truman's ultimate responsibility for foreign policy. Yet, these only prepared the way.

Truman had made an historic decision. He had presented it to Congress in an historic speech. He had used little evidence in the speech, and the logic of relating Greece and Turkey to his doctrine was tortured. Yet, the sweep of his proposal and the fears he aroused created a new Harry Truman.

The transformation was immediately noted. Reporters noticed a new briskness to his step. *Newsweek* reported there was no question now whether he would run for election in his own right or not. His personal approval rating that had stood at 32 percent just after the 1946 congressional elections, now had soared to more than 60 percent. Long stories in major magazines now treated him with greater respect. Before the speech at least one writer had called America's upcoming new global strategy, Marshall's policy. Now and forever more, it would be known as the Truman Doctrine. The increasing prestige accorded to the president gave greater authority to his version of reality and the appropriate ways for Americans to deal with it.

A Brief but Powerful Speech

On May 22, 1947, Truman signed the bill authorizing aid to Greece and Turkey into law. But in the days between February 21 and May 22 much more had happened than a partisan campaign for a political policy. A new reality about the world and America's place in it was announced and began to take hold. The process had begun with Churchill's ["Iron Curtain"] speech but now it had been Americanized and given an enormous boost by Truman's address. Both Churchill and Truman described a world divided into two irreconcilable ideologies. Whereas Churchill called for an alliance, Truman insisted that only the United States was strong enough to engage in this ideological war. The American way of life was at stake. A world hung in the balance. When Secretary Marshall objected to the extravagance of the speech, the reply was that it was the "only way" the president could get Congress to pass the legislation for aid to Greece. That reply suggests that Truman believed the rhetoric pertained only to this situation and that he had Congress in mind as his principal audience. He may have believed that such universal language and commitments were needed on this specific occasion to pass the enabling legislation and that later he could apply these principles selectively. There is considerable evidence that Truman and his advisers did not believe these principles should be applied to Asia, especially China. But Truman underestimated the powerful impact his speech had and the authority he possessed. The drama of the crisis, the melodramatic presentation of arguments, the sinister enemy who was linked to the just defeated but universally hated Nazis—all came together to produce a growing unity among Americans in opposition to communism. Indeed, the rhetorical threat of a diabolical enemy threatening the world all but obscured the policy of sending aid to Greece and Turkey. Bipartisan support from Democrats and Republicans, reinforced by leading journalistic opinion-makers, made it a common reality beyond partisan differences, beyond the president's power to control or recall it. The extensive publicity generated in the press overwhelmed criticism of this new reality. Those who had the fortitude to question or criticize found themselves consigned to the alien community in which questions about their patriotism were raised. In his brief speech President Harry Truman constructed only the bare bones of an American anticommunist ideology. Others would give flesh and muscle to it.

The Truman Doctrine Needlessly Harmed U.S.-Soviet Relations

Roger S. Whitcomb

In the following selection, Roger S. Whitcomb argues that the Truman Doctrine—in which President Truman called for aid to Europe in order to thwart communism—was a poor decision on the president's part. Whitcomb maintains that the doctrine presented an oversimplified view of the world in which Russia represented Communist evil, while America stood for anti-Communist good. He argues that the Truman Doctrine needlessly increased Russian enmity toward the United States and furthered the militarization of the Cold War. Whitcomb is a professor of international relations and foreign policy studies and the director of international studies at Kutztown University in Kutztown, Pennsylvania.

T HE UNFOLDING COLD WAR CONFLICT BETWEEN AMERICA and Russia beginning at the end of World War II was not a simple matter of a conspiracy disguised as a state—Soviet Russia—being confronted by a largely benign and reasonable America. While ideology played an important role in shaping Russia's perceptions of the West, the decision makers in the Kremlin were neither dedicated to nor preoccupied with promoting global revolution. Rather,

Exerpted from *The Cold War in Retrospect: The Formative Years*, by Roger S. Whitcomb. Copyright © 1998 by Roger S. Whitcomb. Reproduced with permission of Greenwood Publishing Group, Inc., Westport, CT.

they were concerned with the security of the Russian state including, above all, a continuing preservation of the power and position of the governing elite.

Russian Security Concerns

Twice in a quarter-century the Russians found themselves faced with a highly destructive German presence in their land, the second time losing over 20 million of their people. They quite naturally were fearful of a resurgence of German (and Japanese) power after 1945. And then there was America, largely untouched by the war and possessed of a monopoly of the atomic capability. Mainly as a result of America's own conduct, Soviet Russia emerged from that conflict unsure of our intentions but, nevertheless, hopeful that the bonds forged during the fighting with the British and Americans would prove to be durable and a basis for postwar peace and cooperation.

While it is true that their Marxist-Leninist ideology imposed itself on their thinking from time to time, especially in regard to their felt need to exploit the "natural" contradictions inherent in the capitalist camp, they nevertheless proceeded essentially from a realpolitik orientation. That this was so is evident when one peruses Russia's conduct in Eastern Europe from 1944–1947. The available evidence indicates that while Moscow desired certain security guarantees and friendly neighbors in Eastern Europe, they in no sense set out to convert the region to Marxism-Leninism as a means to those ends. Consequently, there was a window of opportunity in the immediate postwar period for America and its allies to constructively influence the outcome in places like Poland, Hungary, and Czechoslovakia. Unfortunately, American words and actions themselves exacerbated Russia's deep-seated anxieties, contributing to the intensification (e.g., militarization) of their conflict beginning in 1948.

Perhaps the key mistake made by both America and

Soviet Russia in those initial crucial months after the war was their failure to recognize and explicitly legitimize the essential and bona fide national interests of the other. But this matter, so stated, is not so simple. In America's case, this situation was compounded by the fact that there had never been any clear-cut, unambiguous interest articulated in the first place. It certainly would have been in our national interest to negotiate an explicit quid pro quo with the Russians—one that would have recognized Russian paramount influence in Eastern Europe, and that of America and her allies in Western Europe. But President Truman pursued the worst of all possible courses in that he permitted, de facto, Soviet Russia to exercise hegemony in Eastern Europe while simultaneously refusing to legitimize this process publicly. The result was a monumental misunderstanding with the Kremlin in that each side was perceived as being unwilling to accept the legitimate security interests of the other. Each heard the other to say "no" to their preeminent roles within their own spheres. It was in this context that the unfortunate mirror imagery that came to represent the chief characteristic of postwar Russian-American relations had its origin.

America's Attitude Toward Europe

In looking back at American foreign policy during these years, one must ask why was America so concerned about events in Europe? That, after all, was in contrast with earlier American foreign policy when American security was not deemed to be inextricably linked to that of Europe. The 1940s saw a greatly expanded definition of American interests, drawing on two main lines of thought. First, Hitler's victories seemed to show that Americans could not allow a potential foe to control Western Europe—the leading economic center outside America. If that happened the Western hemisphere might be forced into economic isolation and their security eventually eroded by enemy control of Europe's industrial resources. The decision in July 1946 to fuse the British and American zones of occupation in Germany was made for that reason. In this, the British played an important role in urging America to become more proactive. Without economic recovery, the British feared disaster. Not only would communism increase its appeal among discontented and impoverished people, but the burden of running the zone would become unbearable for Britain's weakened economy. With British and American perceptions in line on the issue, the two governments agreed to fuse their zones.

Linked to this new concern for the European balance was the conviction that air power had revolutionized security. America now needed an extended defense perimeter

Europe During the Cold War

with bases across the Atlantic in Germany and Britain. While these claims had only limited support in 1945–1946, even within the Pentagon, and they were partly advanced for bureaucratic reasons (e.g., to strengthen the case for an air force independent of the army), by 1948–1949 they had become widely accepted within the Administration.

For the Russians the crucial early issue was the settlement of Germany's reparations payments, including substantial amounts from the industrialized western zones controlled by the Allies. In reacting to the stalemate, Washington was initially divided in 1945–1946. The State Department's European Desk, anxious to restore French power, was sympathetic to their arguments, but the War Department and the occupation authorities under General Lucius Clay wanted to get Germany back on its feet economically and end the military regime. Clay's decision to stop reparations payments from the American zone to the Russians (May 1946) was not aimed exclusively at Soviet Russia but was also intended to force the German deadlock to a head in the Allied councils.

Given all of these events, we are now better able to understand the decisive crisis of 1947 [the split between the United States and the Soviet Union as allies]. It was a process of action and reaction in which the primary catalysts came from within Europe. Of particular importance was the abrupt British retreat amid economic crisis in February 1947. Unable to sustain the costs of its overseas commitments, the British were forced to abandon the Palestine mandate, pull out of India, and end financial aid to Greece and Turkey.

What is most puzzling about America's attitude in those initial years after World War II is why the Truman administration thought it important to try to persuade the Russians to sponsor Western-style free elections in Eastern Europe. We were certainly not unaware of the fact that the Balkan states had engaged in provocative anti-Bolshevik policies during the interwar period. It was naive to think that free elections would have resulted in governments friendly to Soviet Russia, as the record of the interwar years so clearly demonstrates. And yet we apparently expected the Kremlin to go ahead and hold such elections—impartial elections that would have in all probability eventuated in regimes likely to pursue tough, anti-Russian policies. Certainly our own record of intervening in the domestic affairs of Caribbean and Central American countries should have given us some sort of appreciation of where Moscow was coming from. Why did we assume that the Russians could be made to extend such an act of forgiveness toward their Western neighbors? And did we really think that legitimate democratic systems could be established in this part of the world—a region whose history of authoritarianism was undeniable?

The Destructive Effect of the Truman Doctrine

This writer has taken the position in [this selection] that the Truman Doctrine was not a constructive contribution to Russian-American relations in the immediate postwar period. Certainly one reason why the Truman Doctrine proved to be so destructive is that it represented in a very real sense the first official manifestation of the Manichean orthodoxy that was to dominate American thinking for the next four decades. This outlook defined the world in terms of a vaguely postulated Russian communist conspiratorial evil, and a vaguely conceived American anti-communist good. [American diplomat George F.] Kennan would later criticize:

> the congenital aversion of Americans to taking specific decisions on specific problems, and by their persistent urge to seek universal formulae or doctrines in which to clothe and justify particular actions. We obviously dislike to discriminate. We like to find some general gov-

erning norm to which, in each instance, appeal can be taken, so that individual decisions may be made not on their particular merits but automatically, depending on whether the circumstances do or do not seem to fit the norm. We like, by the same token, to attribute a universal significance to decisions we have already found it necessary, for limited and parochial reasons, to take.

It is certainly true that the Russians reverted at this time to the sort of inflated and moralist verbal strategy in regard to America (and its capitalist ideology) that had marked their approach at various points in time during the interwar era. Stalin's February 1946 speech was most provocative in this regard, conjuring up old images of inevitable capitalist wars and degeneration. More importantly, and unfortunately, Stalin failed to fully clarify just what specific geophysical arrangements would have been acceptable to Moscow—an initiative that might have served to assuage American concerns regarding the future of Western Europe, the Middle East, and other non-Western zones of potential conflict. Unfortunately, Stalin's expectation of Western enmity was now amply fulfilled by the opposing coalition that his own shortsighted and insensitive moves had helped to provoke. Yet, given the deteriorating political situation between Soviet Russia and America, the inflated tone of Truman's speech must have had an even more devastating impact on Russian perceptions than would have otherwise been the case.

A Utopian Image

One of the more cogent of the critiques of the Truman Doctrine is that it helped to establish a mental outlook in America in which all future crises would be viewed as inherently part and parcel of a worldwide Russian-American struggle. This can be seen over time as Truman's formulation of Russian motives became more and more simplistic and ideological. Whatever Truman's private views about spheres of influence in post–World War II Europe, official American foreign policy by the time of the enunciation of his doctrine reflected a view of the international system as one world, open to democratic values—a world in which the universal ideals of order and stability should prevail— a utopian image, indeed. It was this cognitive outlook, for example, that led American policymakers to perceive the North Korean invasion of South Korea as a Russian-sponsored operation, and, later, to America's involvement in Vietnam as necessary to counteract an "international communist conspiracy."

There can be little doubt, of course, that Truman's perception of American public opinion at this time influenced the way he couched his speech before the Congress. Gaddis and others point out that the domestic political situation dictated the kind of verbal strategy that Truman and his chief lieutenants adopted at this time. The Republicans were in control of the Congress, and many of them were still unreconstructed isolationists—a mood set that reflected the attitudes of many of their constituents. Having "brought the boys home from Europe," it would certainly have been difficult to even consider a reversal of the demobilization policies of those immediate postwar months. Shock therapy was required.

A Foreign Policy Milestone

And so Washington found it necessary to administer "the adrenalin of great anxiety" ([Dean] Acheson's phrase) into the public forum because it was feared that the American people could not be sufficiently galvanized by measured intellectual analysis to achieve the strengthening of Western power. Thus, the Doctrine was designed to "prod Congress and the American people into accepting the responsibilities of world leadership." In so doing, the Doctrine, not coincidentally, turned out to be the first successful salvo in a long process of reversing the recent postwar shift of power and responsibility in foreign affairs to the Congress—a transformation that would lead to what Arthur Schlesinger would later call the "imperial presidency."

The Doctrine was a milestone for several other reasons, not the least of which was that this was the first time in the postwar era that America substantively intervened in another country's civil war. As such, the Greek intervention was the prototype in a long series of such initiatives—all to be justified as part and parcel of necessarily large aid programs to prevent the collapse of "free world" economies and institutions. Yet, when all was said and done, the intervention in Greece succeeded only because Tito withdrew his aid for the communist guerrillas as a result of his expulsion from the communist party bloc in 1948. It was still a close call, putting America at the brink of military intervention.

Finally, the Doctrine was based implicitly on the domino theory approach—on the assumption that Stalin, like Hitler, by way of analogy, was intent on unlimited conquest. Only raising a wall would suffice to dam the red tide. Perhaps the most lasting and deleterious consequence was that from 1947 onward any threats to the West's political-economic well-being could be easily explained as communist-inspired, not as problems that arose from difficulties inherent in the international order itself.

The Marshall Plan Helped Save Europe's Economy

Theodore A. Wilson

On June 5, 1947, Truman's secretary of state, George Marshall, gave the commencement speech at Harvard University in which he set forth the idea of the European Recovery Program (ERP), more popularly known as the Marshall Plan. The plan was devised to help Europe recover economically from World War II and entailed the United States providing more than 12 billion dollars in aid to Europe. Theodore A. Wilson writes in the following essay that, contrary to the views of its critics, the Marshall Plan was successful in saving the European economy. According to Wilson, the Marshall Plan led to an increase in industrial and agricultural production and dramatically boosted the self-confidence of the Western European nations that had been badly damaged during World War II. Wilson concedes that the Truman administration was unable to unify Europe but argues that the Marshall Plan must be considered an overall success. Wilson is the director of the Hall Center for the Humanities and a professor of history at the University of Kansas in Lawrence.

A N ASSESSMENT OF THE ORIGINAL SPAN OF THE MARSHALL Plan, during which most of the goals that had been projected for four or more years were realized, reveals that

Excerpted from "The Marshall Plan: 1947–1951," by Theodore A. Wilson, *Headline Series*, no. 236 (1977). Reprinted by permission of the Foreign Policy Association, New York, www.fpa.org.

the achievements of the program were enormous by any standard. To the nations which formed the Organization for European Economic Corporation (OEEC), the United States gave, via the Marshall Plan, the sum of $13,348,800,000. Nearly three-quarters of the total went to five countries: Britain ($3,189,800,000), France ($2,713,600,000), Italy ($1,508,800,000), West Germany ($1,390,600,000) and the Netherlands ($982,100,000).

It was a magnificent effort, despite all the problems, and the effects on Europe's economic vitality were striking. Industrial production in Western Europe in 1950 was 45 percent higher than in 1947, and 25 percent higher than in 1938. By 1952 European industries were churning out goods at a rate 200 percent above that of 1938. Perhaps even more important was the increase in agricultural output, up 15 percent over 1938. "In human terms," Paul Hoffman observed, "Europeans were eating, they had jobs, they were working and working hard." And though certain basic weaknesses in Europe's economic structure were not eradicated, much progress was made. For example, the dollar gap, which once had been considered beyond the capacity of Europe to correct, was reduced by some 80 percent.

With these economic achievements went organizational steps which, however limited, were nonetheless historic. In 1948 and 1949 major steps were taken to liberalize intra-European trade. In 1950 the European Payments Union was formed to facilitate currency exchange and rectify payments imbalances. In 1952 came the launching of the Coal and Steel Community, from which the Common Market evolved.

The Marshall Plan Had a Revolutionary Impact

The psychological impact of the Marshall Plan appears to have been nothing less than revolutionary. In 1947 Europe had been stagnating. Marshall's simple words brought renewed hope. For British Foreign Secretary Ernest Bevin, the Marshall Plan "was like a lifeline to sinking men. It seemed to bring hope when there was none. The generosity of it was beyond belief. . . . I think you can understand why, therefore, we responded with such alacrity and why we grabbed the lifeline with both hands, as it were." In just a few months after Marshall's speech there was a new spirit abroad throughout Western Europe. There was renewed faith in the capacity of democratic institutions to deal with economic and social problems. The "economic miracle" that transformed the rubble-strewn landscape of occupied Germany into a bustling, prosperous industrial giant resulted from the revival of the German people's faith in the future. France, Italy, Britain and other OEEC nations experienced a similar return of self-confidence.

The Marshall Plan greatly helped to stem the spread of Communist ideology and Russian influence. The return of economic vitality stabilized the political climate throughout Western Europe and brought once weak governments solidly into the anti-Communist camp. By 1952 there existed a solid foundation on which the United States and co-operating nations could attempt to build an alliance against the U.S.S.R. Such an effort would have been impossible at the time the Marshall Plan first was announced in 1947.

Hailing the Marshall Plan as "one of the great success stories of all time," Harry Bayard Price, the official historian of the program, wrote in 1955:

> It furnished a counterpoise to the forces of aggression. In so doing, it probably forestalled a collapse of Western Europe and the Mediterranean area and their unwilling incorporation into the orbit of world communism. It afforded without stint the critical margin of resources and energy needed to make possible an amazingly rapid recuperation of the European economy. . . . It demonstrated, in unprecedented fashion, the possibility of organizing and carrying out vast international endeavors—not for destruction, but for construction and

peace. Belying in performance the charge of imperialism, it gave the United States a new stature as a leader to be trusted. And it set in train a succession of promising developments. Could more be asked of a single venture?

Not a Failure

For many years historians refrained from asking anything more from the ERP. Viewing it through the lens of cold war antagonisms, they presented it only as a necessary act to restore economic health and thus political equilibrium to Europe. In recent years, however, some scholars have asked different questions about U.S. initiatives such as the Marshall Plan, and they have written unfavorably about both its purposes and its achievements. For example, in their massive study of postwar American diplomacy [*The Limits of Power: The World and United States Foreign Policy, 1945–1954*], Joyce and Gabriel Kolko entitle a central chapter, "The Failure of the Marshall Plan." The Kolkos argue that even in terms of its proclaimed goals (ensuring European recovery, building a wall against Soviet aggression) the ERP was monumentally unsuccessful. It served to return to power those "reactionary *status quo* oriented elements" with whom the United States preferred to deal, but it failed to bring a better life to the vast majority of Europeans. Thus, it intensified the political instability and social alienation that already dominated European life. "There was no longer any doubt in early 1950," the Kolkos write, "about the direction of both the American and European economies, nor about the original goals that Washington desired." Such claims, in the writer's view, exaggerate both the immoral purposes and the foresight of the U.S. government. To put forward the proposition that the Truman Administration was pursuing a cold, calculated strategy to fasten American economic domination on Western Europe is a profound distortion of what did, in fact, take place.

Indeed, it can be argued that the "failures" of the Marshall Plan were the result of the reluctance of its advocates to press with sufficient determination for its basic goals. It may be that a golden opportunity was allowed to slip away during the dark days of 1947 to 1949. "Don't you see," a former OEEC official once complained to the author in the course of an interview, "we were all in the same boat in 1947. And the boat was sinking fast. There was no concern about butter surpluses and pork quotas. We all needed everything and only the United States could supply our needs. The situation made possible changes of revolutionary import. But we could not and would not make these hard decisions of our own volition. Had the United States exerted strong pressure, amounting to blackmail, had you said, 'Our aid is conditional upon immediate and significant changes. Reform your tax systems, abolish all discriminatory trade arrangements, take concrete steps toward the integration of European economic life,' I think we would have agreed."

Certainly, many Americans understood the potential power they wielded over Western Europe. As Averell Harriman wrote Paul G. Hoffman in November 1948, "The ECA [Economic Cooperation Administration] has a big stick which can mean either life or disaster to many European countries and their people." But one searches without success for evidence that the U.S. government ever engaged in blackmail to achieve its goals. It was not done to achieve land reform to Italy or abolition of France's crazy-quilt tax structure or any of numerous other desperately needed changes. Indeed, instances of "reverse blackmail"—Britain exploiting its special relationship with the United States to get its way in the OEEC, France using its political instability to extort funds for the war in Indochina—were much more common.

The Integration Failure

The inability of the Truman Administration to pressure Europe into integration is exemplified by the long, exhausting debate over the issue. The ERP offered a great, perhaps unique, opportunity, as Georges Bidault observed, "to construct a Europe, not . . . against other nations . . . but to put an end to a state of anarchy which gives rise to conflicts by maintaining distress." It might have accomplished a reordering of European values, the rationalization of Western Europe's economic life and the removal of all barriers to peaceful cooperation between the nations of Europe. A start might even have been made toward achievement of that age-old dream, political union. The United States was determined to have this start made. American representatives—from Hoffman and Harriman to the most junior clerk in ECA's field offices—preached integration. More time and energy was devoted to this issue in the councils of ECA and the OEEC than was given to any other question. In the end, however, the unification of Europe stopped halfway. Opposition by some member nations, especially Britain, slowed its growth in the early days of the Marshall Plan. Then, the shift to military cooperation removed integration as a viable issue.

Why the United States did not use its leverage to force integration is open to various explanations: belief that such blatant interference in the internal affairs of other nations was both politically risky and immoral; the violent opposition of the British, for whom many Americans possessed a peculiar regard and deference; and fear on the part of Treasury planners and others that a united Europe would end their dream of global economic integration. Fear of a European reaction was probably uppermost. Also important was lack of agreement about the need to take such risks. "The conception of recovery held by many," one planner later reflected, "was a limited conception of simply getting Europe back on its feet. This conception was sold to Congress. The reality, however, was that Europe was not on its feet before the war. The recovery conception was therefore mistaken—but there it was." As a result, the impasse over

European integration was never broken. A habit of post-poning whatever did not seem urgent (no matter how important in the long run)—that weakness which had long afflicted U.S. foreign policy—was permitted to prevail.

From Economic to Military Assistance

It is unfair to describe the shift from economic to military assistance as a "failure" on the part of those who created and administered the Marshall Plan. As noted earlier, changing circumstances produced an apparently irresistible tide in favor of a military response to Europe's

---

Lessons of the Marshall Plan

Walt W. Rostow, a professor of political economy at the University of Texas at Austin, explains that although the Marshall Plan cannot be implemented in the modern world, its principles should serve as guidelines for future foreign policy decisions.

As the world faces the challenges of the next half-century, it must remember that the Marshall Plan was the right policy for its time and place but that those circumstances are not likely to recur. The success of the Marshall Plan has generated the false hope that the application of capital and technology could do for Third World countries, inner cities, and post-communist Eastern Europe what was achieved in Western Europe in the wake of World War II. Unlike these areas, Western Europe did not need to be invented, it simply had to be recalled. With its skilled and educated work force, its market experience, and its mature political structures, modern Europe is not easy to replicate. At their best, the developing countries, such as South Korea and Taiwan, took two or three decades to catch up with the advanced industrialized world. At the other end of the spectrum, sub-Saharan Africa has not mounted a takeoff after more than 30 years of

problems. Events in China, Korea and Southeast Asia, the Berlin Blockade and the first Russian explosion of an atomic bomb in September 1949 gave anxiety to Congress and the American people. It is therefore understandable that proposals to set up a defensive system in Europe (rather than at the continental limits of the United States) proved so appealing.

In retrospect, however, the necessity for that complex, burdensome and arguably inadequate instrument that NATO became can be challenged. The difficulties facing Western Europe were as much psychological as economic,

independence. . . .

The world will require a new political economy to deal with the strains imposed by the full industrialization of the developing states, and the stagnant or falling birth rates and aging populations of the older industrialized states and the more precocious developing countries. This is not the occasion to lay out comprehensive thoughts on how to deal with the problems of the next century. But the political structure of the Marshall Plan embodied two principles that bear on them directly.

First, political support in the United States for the Marshall Plan was bipartisan and embraced most of the country's major interests. The United States should face the truly revolutionary problems that the next century will bring with an equally bipartisan and broad-based foundation. Second, the Marshall Plan's program was not worked out bilaterally by the United States and the individual countries of Europe but multilaterally. . . . In the 21st century, the diffusion of power makes it even more essential that plans of action be arrived at on a multilateral basis.

Walt W. Rostow, *Foreign Affairs*, May/June 1997.

political or military. The need, as originally conceived, was to restore the faith of Europeans in themselves and their institutions. Had the architects of the Marshall Plan kept faith with this original conception, the further intensification of the cold war which occurred with the creation of NATO might have been avoided, and the energies of one of Europe's ablest leaders, instead of being diverted into military affairs, could have been retained for the work of European political and economic progress.

That this did not happen resulted from failure to provide either friends or enemies with what Dean Acheson once termed "communicable wisdom" regarding U.S. purposes. The actual purposes of the Marshall Plan were never made wholly explicit. In part, this was because of the role of the U.S. Congress. The process by which the Marshall Plan was "sold" to Congress made it inevitable that the aid program that ultimately emerged would only partly respond to Europe's true needs and America's actual capabilities. The Truman Administration, as was necessary, exploited congressional prejudices in order to push through the ERP; but it found itself, as a result, forced to overlay the hard facts about Europe's problems with simplistic arguments that conformed to these prejudices. Exaggerated claims and emphasis on the superficial, Acheson once complained, "is what happens to plans when they get into the congressional mill. Something happens all along the line. . . . Everything has to be stepped up a little bit to get the attention of people who are more interested in rivers and harbors than in foreign affairs, so that things are put in a much more critical situation than we would want to do." It may have been necessary to play this game. However, as a result, the Marshall Plan was vulnerable to charges that it had not brought the American version of the good life to all Europeans, converted every last French and Italian Communist into a Rotarian, and accomplished all the other miracles its supporters had promised. Such complaints reflected not so much on the Marshall Plan as on the prevailing American ignorance of the realities of international politics.

Why the Marshall Plan Succeeded

Despite such reservations, we must conclude that the Marshall Plan was successful. Even if it did not lead immediately to a United States of Europe or to sweeping structural reforms of Western European society, even though ERP was not permitted to complete its original task, it did restore European self-confidence and demonstrated that the problems engulfing Europe were not beyond solution. The Marshall Plan provided an enormous psychological lift for both Western Europe and the United States.

The reasons why the Marshall Plan succeeded against such long odds are not really complicated, though the circumstances were complex and are, to some degree, still unexplained. Any list of the "success factors" would include, first, the simplicity and appropriateness of the idea undergirding the Marshall Plan. Its conception was a creative act, one which met a deep need and captured the imagination of millions. Europe desperately needed help. The United States was in a position to provide this assistance and found the means to do so.

A second factor was the energy, not to say daring, with which the conception was carried through. Americans looked realistically and clearly at an international crisis, and the response ushered in a new era in U.S. policy toward the world. The Marshall Plan idea was put forward despite the political risks at home and the uncertain situation in Europe. It was statesmanlike not only because it was courageous but because it appealed to the highest instincts of all those involved. It promised dignity and self-respect to Europeans, and it asked of Americans that sense of responsibility and realism which had long been missing in U.S. diplomacy.

Third, and perhaps most important in the long run, the Marshall Plan was accorded broad public discussion. The American people and Congress for once participated in the making of policy instead of being asked to engage in postmortems about past errors in the realm of foreign affairs. Thus, the process of public debate was constructive rather than destructive, and the American people obtained full knowledge about an initiative which they were asked to support and for which, ultimately, they had to pay the bill. It is only unfortunate that this widespread enthusiasm and understanding could not be sustained throughout the Marshall Plan's existence.

A fourth factor, referred to earlier, was the quality of the men and women recruited to direct and administer the program. High morale and a sense of dedication were characteristic of the ECA for much of the program's life. The era of the Marshall Plan established a standard which all subsequent aid agencies (and many other organizations as well) have sought to emulate. Perhaps the strongest evidence of the abilities of the ECA staff and of their counterparts in Europe is the distinction so many have since achieved in public service, academic life, the professions and business. The roll call of former Marshall Plan personnel, both to Europe and the United States, includes many of the most distinguished figures of the past quarter-century.

Fifth, it is important to note that the organizations established put into effect the aims of the Marshall Plan— the ECA and the OEEC—were especially well designed to accomplish their principal goals. In the long-standing debate over the advantages of adapting an existing agency to new circumstances and responsibilities as contrasted with creating a new one—a temporary, special-purpose instrument to meet particular needs—the Marshall Plan provides powerful testimony to the value of the latter course. Also important was the unusual latitude given the ECA in carrying out its responsibilities. Not since that time has an "independent" agency been so independent.

Sixth is the related issue of the Marshall Plan's capacity to adjust to changing circumstances and needs. Although there were limits to its flexibility, the ERP did evolve, and the successive stages in its evolution were essential to the success of the program.

Finally, and almost impossible to document, must be mentioned the spirit of the Marshall Plan. The sense of its rightness for the time and place of its creation takes in all of the above factors. For those who participated, however, the spirit of the Marshall Plan was and is a transcendent reality.

The Marshall Plan Did Not Improve the European Economy

Jeffrey Tucker

In the following selection, Jeffrey Tucker disputes the argument that the Marshall Plan, under which the United States dispensed over $12 billion in aid to Europe between 1948 and 1951, saved the European economy. He writes that the nations that received little or no Marshall Plan aid showed greater improvements in their economy than the nations that were assisted. Tucker argues that the real beneficiaries of the plan were the American corporations that sent goods to Europe and were able to entrench themselves in those overseas markets. Truman only supported the plan, according to Tucker, because he hoped it would bolster his political popularity. Tucker concludes that the Marshall Plan had little impact on the Western European economy, which only improved after the plan ran its course and elements of the free market—ending price controls and curbing the power of unions—were implemented. Tucker is the editor of *Free Market*.

THE 50TH ANNIVERSARY OF THE MARSHALL PLAN provided another occasion for the media to celebrate the government's good works. The U.S.'s headlong plunge into global welfarism (nearly $100 billion in current dollars), they said, saved European economies after the Second

Reprinted, with permission, from "The Marshall Plan Myth," by Jeffrey Tucker, *Free Market*, September 1997.

World War. One reporter, Garrick Utley of NBC, even theorized that Marshall aid explains why East Germany was poor and West Germany rich.

As economist Tyler Cowen has noted, the countries that received the most Marshall Plan money (allies Britain, Sweden, and Greece) grew the slowest between 1947 and 1955, while those that received the least money (axis powers Germany, Austria, and Italy) grew the most. In terms of post-war prosperity, then, it eventually paid to be a political enemy of the U.S. instead of a "beneficiary" of international charity.

The Real Purpose of the Marshall Plan

But this truth is only news if you think that the Marshall Plan was genuinely intended to help foreign countries. But as with all government programs, it pays returns to look beneath the surface. So what exactly was the point of the Marshall Plan, named for General George Marshall? It's been well-described in the works of historians William Appleman Williams, Gabriel Kolko, Stephen Ambrose, and Alan Milward.

Marshall himself played the role of a patsy, delivering prepackaged speeches written by the players behind the plan. His original pitch, given at Harvard, was for money to end "hunger, poverty, desperation, and chaos." But the real upshot of the Marshall Plan was a political maneuver to loot American taxpayers to keep influential American corporations on the government dole. The Plan's legacy was the egregious and perpetual use of foreign aid for domestic political and economic purposes.

After the war ended, Harry Truman's popularity in the polls began to plummet, as did the prestige of government generally. The American people had made huge sacrifices to fight the war and now wanted curbs in government, which had been administering a centrally planned economy. Most of all, they wanted the foreign policy recommended by George Washington and Thomas Jefferson: trade with all, entanglements with none.

In the mainstream of thinking was Republican Senator Robert Taft, a hero of all free-market activists at the time. He demanded tax cuts, spending cuts, and an end to "constantly increasing interference with family life and with business by autocratic government bureaus and autocratic labor leaders." The Republican party swept midterm elections in 1946, taking back the Congress on a hard-core, anti-big government platform.

Truman had to do something big and he knew it. As Charles Mee reports, he needed "some large program that would let him recapture the initiative, something big enough to enable him to gather in all the traditional factions of the Democratic Party and also some middle-of-the-road Republicans, and at the same time, something that would hamper the Republican phalanx," and establish him as a world leader.

Truman and His Co-Conspirators

The issue was right before him: foreign aid, funneled through the corporate establishment and cloaked in the rhetoric of opposition to foreign (but not domestic) communism. Cynically, he would make good use of Russia, which only the day before had been our gallant ally in the war, and transform it into a monster that had to be destroyed. By stealing the Republicans' anti-socialist rhetoric, Truman hoped to frazzle his opponents and make himself a hero on the world stage.

Truman had plenty of co-conspirators, men who have gone down in history as the architects of the original New World Order. Fabled establishmentarians Averell Harriman and Charles Kindleberger were central figures. But it was Dean Acheson, undersecretary of state and the most menacing statist of the immediate post-war era, who concocted the plan to make the wartime empire permanent. Acheson persuaded Navy secretary James Forrestal and domestic fixer Clark Clifford to show Truman how he could elevate a political scam like foreign aid into a mighty ideological struggle on the global stage.

A little-known business group, founded in 1942 and called the Committee for Economic Development, was elevated into a think tank for a new international order—the economic counterpart to the Council on Foreign Relations. The Committee's founders were the heads of the top steel, automotive, and electric industries who had benefitted from the New Deal's corporatist statism. Its membership overlapped with the farther left National Planning Association, which was unabashedly national socialist in ideological orientation.

These groups understood that they owed their profit margins to government subsidies provided by the New Deal and wartime production subsidies. Faced with postwar peace, they feared a future in which they would be forced to compete on a free-market basis. Their personal and institutional security was at stake, so they got busy dreaming up strategies to sustain a profitable statism in a peacetime economy.

Corporate economic interests, then, overlapped with Truman's political interests, and an unholy alliance between business and government was born. They would use Europe's miseries to line their own pockets in the name of "rebuilding" and providing "security" against trumped-up threats to American security.

The Example of Greece

The test case came in 1947 with aid to Greece, where a communist party was making electoral advances. Truman saw the main chance, and demanded $400 million in foreign aid, which Congress approved as a swipe against Russia. Just as the money was being channeled to special-interest groups, however, members of Congress learned that the "Russian connection" to the Greek communist party had been phonied up. As it turned out, Greece, like every European country, just wanted the cash.

Even so, the political success of the Truman doctrine of global giveaways had been demonstrated, and the script for billions in future giveaways had been written. Over the next five years, "Marshall money" would corrupt nearly every Christian democratic party in Europe, turning them into carbon copies of the U.S. democratic party. Those political parties in turn worked to create monstrous welfare states and regulatory controls that continue to hinder European economic growth today.

On the heels of the success in Greece, Dean Acheson formed an ad hoc committee to find "situations elsewhere in the world" that "may require analogous, technical, and

The True Cause of West Germany's Recovery

Tyler Cowen, a professor of economics at George Mason University in Fairfax, Virginia, argues that West Germany had begun its postwar economic recovery before the implementation of the Marshall Plan.

The German economic recovery is the most miraculous example of European postwar economic growth and the most frequently cited example of a Marshall Plan success. Thus, it deserves a closer look.

American aid never exceeded 5 percent of West Germany's GNP, even in 1948–49, at the height of ECA assistance. At the same time, Allied occupation costs and reparations absorbed from 11 to 15 percent of West Germany's GNP. The US government's policies, therefore, *caused* German resource problems rather than cured them. The net economic transfers out of West Germany loom even larger because throughout the mid-1950s Bonn repaid half of its ECA aid. . . .

military aid on our part." With no effort, the ad hoc committee was able to classify most of Europe as in need of economic aid. The committee found shortages of just about everything, and, in particular, dollars to buy goods from corporate America. A mythical "dollar shortage" (as if trade is only possible with a world awash in paper) was the crisis of the moment.

But beneath the surface, the true objective was the internationalization of the New Deal, a bureaucrat's dream. As Julius Krug, secretary of the interior, said in his memoirs, the Marshall Plan, "essential to our own continued productivity and prosperity," was a Tennessee Valley Authority on a world scale. "It is as if we were building a TVA every Tuesday."

West Germany's upturn really began on June 20, 1948, when the Allies instituted currency reform, effectively "teething" the money supply; that is, bringing the money supply to one-tenth its initial level. The old Reichsmark became a Deutschemark in one of the most drastic deflations ever. The average German's standard of living shot up within hours of the currency reform as people became fully willing to accept currency in return for goods and services.

Less than one month later, Ludwig Erhard, German economic director of Bizonia (the postwar American-British occupation zone), pushed the German economy further onto the right track. One Sunday, when everyone else had left their offices, Erhard defied orders and issued an edict abolishing most of the Allied economic controls. . . .

Erhard's free-market philosophy worked well. Monthly production indices rose at rates that exceeded many later *yearly* increases. The West German economic miracle was underway. Several months later, Marshall Plan aid began to arrive.

Tyler Cowen, *Reason*, April 1986.

Yet even after the Greece vote, polls showed tremendous public opposition to any foreign giveaways. In one meeting, the Republican House Majority Leader Charles Halleck told Truman flat out: "You must realize there is a growing resistance to these programs. I have been out on the hustings, and I know. The people don't like it."

The Role of Corporations in the Marshall Plan

The Truman gang had already thought of that. Months before the vote, he brought together the heads of major corporations to enlist them in the cause. Members of this organizing committee, drawn from the Committee for Economic Development, included, most prominently, Hiland Vatcheller, president of the Allegheny-Ludlum Steel Corporation; W. Randolph Burgess, vice-chairman of National City Bank of New York; Paul G. Hoffmann, president of Studebaker Corp. (and later administrator of Marshall funds), as well as the secretary treasurers of the AFL and the CIO.

Leading the corporate charge for secure profits was Will Clayton, the Texas cotton impresario whose business was about to experience a remarkable tax-subsidized boom. The last world war had already made his company the second largest cotton-trading company in the world. Unlike his competitors during the New Deal, while working with Franklin Delano Roosevelt (FDR) to wreck the American economy, he was smart enough to move his operations to Brazil, Mexico, Paraguay, and Egypt. By the Second World War, he was selling 15 percent of the world cotton crop.

As the war ended, he reenlisted in the campaign for the home front. As undersecretary of state for economic affairs in 1947, Clayton too saw the main chance. "Let us admit right off," he said in defense of the idea of foreign aid: "We need markets—big markets—in which to buy and sell." Here is the core truth of all such aid. The intent is not to help foreign countries; it is to reward home-based multi-nationals who actually get the cash as the government purchases political influence abroad.

Nothing was left to chance. Acheson worked with the established corporate elites and the State Department to create a supposed grass-roots organization called "Citizens' Committee for the Marshall Plan." As many as one thousand speakers representing the group toured the country to whip up support. It also ghost-wrote Congressional testimony from other organizations on behalf of the aid package. As Averell Harriman told several European ambassadors during a visit to the British embassy, they haven't seen anything compared with the "flood of organized propaganda which the Administration is about to unloose."

It was left to Will Clayton to make the economic case. Perversely, he touted the Marshall Plan as the triumph of "free enterprise." Moreover, he said, if communism comes to Europe, "I think the situation which we would face in this country would be a very grave one." We would "have to reorder and readjust our whole economy in this country if we lost the European market."

In the days before the vote, the claims became more extreme and, with the media-corporate-banking-government elite on board, the propaganda became ever more hysterical. We were told that a depression would come. The U.S. would be bombed. We'd be in another war if the aid package failed. The situation is as bleak as it was for France in 1938. American life as we know it would end forthwith.

When the plan passed, as it easily did (with even Taft's vote), the ink was hardly dry on the legislation when the ships full of goods hit the high seas. At any given moment over the next few months, 150 boats were carrying wheat, flour, cotton, tires, borax, drilling equipment, tractors, tobacco, aircraft parts, and anything else big domestic manufacturers could get their hands on.

Further Corporate Advantages

As with most goods shipped under the Marshall Plan, American producers had the advantage: 50 percent had to be sent on American vessels. Oil exports to Europe exploded even as imports from Europe were cut by one-third. In aid distribution, there was bias in favor of finished goods, to prevent European businesses from competing with American producers on down the production line.

Taking a leaf from the Roosevelt playbook, Truman bypassed the usual bureaucracy and established a new bureau—the Economic Cooperative Administration—to distribute the aid. It too was staffed by the heads of major industrial-corporate interests who stood to benefit at public expense. Paul Hoffman headed the group and passed out billions to well-heeled corporate powers. As historian Anthony Carew summarizes, the Marshall Plan "was in all major respects a business organization run by businessmen." (Hoffman later became head of the far-left Ford Foundation.)

Most of all, the aid was used for purchases at distorted prices by American tax dollars in the hands of European governments. The mad scramble for tax dollars was a disgrace to behold, creating a low point in U.S. business history. Time and again, Congress intervened to grant corporate America what it really wanted: restrictions that forced Marshall aid to go to purchases of American oil, aluminum, wood, textiles, and machines.

The aid was also used to directly subsidize particular firms in recipient countries, whether or not there were viable markets for their products. Instead, the firms received money because their continued existence would artificially support "full employment" policies. And since American labor union groups were intimately involved in choosing who got the money, the lion's share went to companies with closed union shops, paradoxically restricting the ability of labor markets to readjust to new economic realities.

From an economic perspective, the Marshall Plan was modeled on a static view of investment. Countries were asked what their present needs were and the U.S. responded. Not a thought was given to the possibility that economic growth alone would provide. It eventually did, but only after the Marshall Plan welfare was cut off and domestic manufacturers were able to find markets for their products.

The result was the largest peacetime transfer of wealth from the taxpayers to corporations until that point in U.S. history. And it wasn't only dollars that were exported. Through a massive and tax-funded "technical expertise program," European businesses came to the U.S. to take lessons in management practices, visiting mostly unionized automobile companies, electric utility plants, and huge farm operations—the most socialistic of U.S. sectors.

The Legacy of the Marshall Plan

All told, the Marshall Plan dumped $13 billion, or nearly $100 billion in today's dollars. It was enough to firmly entrench American companies in European markets, especially in Britain, France, and Germany. American-controlled companies dominated industries such as shoes, milk, cereals, machines, cars, canned goods, petroleum refinement, locks and keys, printing, tires, soaps, clocks, farm machinery, and much more.

These were mere bubbles of prosperity, forced investment created through insider deals of the worst sort. Indeed, Hoffman worked under the constant fear that the racketeering would come to the surface. He feared some enterprising journalist might expose the entire thing, hearings would follow, and the plan would be discredited. That never happened.

A year after the Marshall Plan began sucking private capital out of the economy, the U.S. fell into recession, precisely the opposite of what its proponents predicted. Meanwhile, the aid did not help Europe. What reconstructed Europe was the post-Marshall freeing up of controlled prices, keeping inflation in check, and curbing union power—that is, the free market. As even Hoffman admitted in his memoir, the aid did not in fact help the economies of Europe. The primary benefit was "psychological." Expensive therapy, indeed.

The actual legacy of the Marshall Plan was a vast expansion of government at home, the beginnings of the Cold War rhetoric that would sustain the welfare-warfare state for 40 years, a permanent global troop presence, and an entire business class on the take from Washington. It also created a belief on the part of the ruling elite in D.C. that it could trick the public into backing anything, including the idea that government and its connected interest groups should run the world at taxpayer expense.

Truman Handled the Berlin Crisis Cautiously

Avi Shlaim

At the end of World War II, Berlin was divided by sectors, with each sector controlled by one of the Allies—the Soviet Union, Britain, France, and the United States. In March 1948, the latter three nations decided to unify their sectors. A few months later, the Soviets began a blockade between Berlin and the West and announced on June 24, 1948, that the Allies no longer had power in Berlin. Two days later, the United States and Britain began an airlift to provide West Berlin with food and other needed supplies; that airlift would last eleven months, until the blockade was lifted.

In the following essay, Avi Shlaim explains that both domestic and foreign policy concerns led to Truman's cautious decision to implement the airlift rather than attempt to break the blockade through military force. In the summer of 1948, Truman's popularity in America was at a low and his prospects for reelection looked shaky. Consequently, Shlaim writes, Truman viewed the Berlin crisis as a way to strengthen his image by being resolute toward the Soviets. Though the president wanted to take a stand against the Soviet blockade, he also wanted to avoid any action that could lead to war. Shlaim is an historian and Professor of International Relations at St. Antony's, Oxford University.

T HE SEVERANCE BY THE SOVIET AUTHORITIES OF ALL LAND communications between Berlin and the Western

Excerpted from *The United States and the Berlin Blockade, 1948-1949: A Study in Crisis Decision Making*, by Avi Shlaim. Copyright © 1983 by The Regents of the University of California. Reprinted by permission of University of California Press.

zones on June 24, 1948, marked the beginning of the crisis period. This action triggered all three necessary conditions for crisis: a sharp rise in threat perception, an awareness of time constraints on decisions, and an image of the higher probability of war. The crisis period continued until July 22, when the proposal for an armed convoy to break the blockade was rejected and the decision was taken to expand the airlift. As a result, time pressure declined in intensity, marking the beginning of a much larger post-crisis period.

The key decision-makers during the Berlin crisis period were President Truman, Secretary [of State George] Marshall, and General [Lucius P.] Clay. The rise in threat perception, time constraints, and probability of war brought the President to the center of the policymaking arena. Indecision in Washington, however, left Clay ample scope, which he utilized fully, to influence the American response. As in the pre-crisis period, a number of other decision-makers participated alongside the three key figures in the decision process. Prominent in this second group were Secretary of Defense James Forrestal, Secretary of the Army Kenneth Royall, Under Secretary of the Army William Draper, Under Secretary of State Robert Lovett, and the State Department's representative in Germany, Robert Murphy. . . .

Truman and Foreign Policy

Throughout the crisis period, Truman was deeply preoccupied with domestic politics. He had already entered the 1948 presidential campaign to secure a second term in the White House. To dispel the widespread gloom and pessimism in the Democratic camp about his prospects for re-election, Truman went on an extended tour in June to address people directly in all parts of the country. Yet, almost unanimously, the polls taken before the 1948 Democratic convention showed that his popularity with the American people had hit an all-time low. Even some of his closest friends and advisers were counseling him to change his mind about going after the nomination.

The 1948 Presidential Election

Truman's insecure domestic political base, coupled with his ambition to have a second term as President, weighed heavily on his conduct of foreign policy. With the Democratic convention coming up on July 12, he preferred to postpone any public action on the Berlin blockade. He refrained from making any comments on it at news conferences and instructed Clay not to make statements referring to the possibility of war over Berlin. But he was far from being oblivious to the opportunity offered by the Berlin crisis for restoring his sagging electoral fortunes. The American public apparently made one primary demand of American foreign policy: that it be firm and resolute in its opposition to Soviet expansion. Truman's greatest asset was his control over foreign policy, which provided opportunities for demonstrating that he could satisfy this requirement. This asset was taken into account in planning Truman's 1948 campaign strategy. "There is considerable political advantage to the Administration in its battle with the Kremlin," wrote Clark Clifford in a memorandum outlining this strategy. But only, he emphasized, "up to a certain point—the real danger of imminent war." Clifford also advised Truman to emerge more forcefully and dramatically as the architect of the containment policy, so that the American people would identify the tough line against Russia with the President personally. Truman's handling of the Berlin crisis suggests that he heeded this advice and, in particular, that he appreciated the importance of not carrying the contest with the Kremlin to the point where war became an imminent danger.

After securing the Democratic nomination for the Presidency on July 14, Truman had to contend with two rivals: on his left he had Henry Wallace, the leader of the Progressive Party, who attributed the blockade to the aggressive Cold War policies of the Truman Administration and recommended withdrawal from Berlin; on his right he had Thomas Dewey, the Republican candidate, who was appealing for a tougher stand against Russia. Truman shrewdly sensed that the American public would support a firm policy which stopped short of raising the risk of war. By following a middle course, he was able to deflect the charges of bellicosity and the charges of weakness directed at him from the left and the right, respectively. This middle course also enabled Truman, as Clifford had urged him, to consolidate his image as the real architect of containment and as a national leader who could be relied upon to stand up to the Russians abroad and defend America's vital interests without acting provocatively or recklessly.

The Berlin Dilemma

But while Truman was as skillful as Franklin Roosevelt in using foreign policy for partisan advantage, it would be misleading to depict him as a politician who was solely concerned with partisan advantage. Images and perceptions pertaining to the external environment were no less important in conditioning Truman's conduct during the crisis period. The Berlin blockade presented the President with one of the most acute dilemmas of the Cold War era. If he resorted to force to break the blockade, he might touch off World War III. If he failed to take any action and withdrew from the city under duress, America's policy in Germany and Europe would suffer a major, possibly fatal, setback.

Division of opinion among Truman's advisers on the feasibility and wisdom of maintaining the Western position in Berlin did not make the task any easier. At the inception of the blockade, Berlin was not unequivocally accepted by all senior officials as vital to American interests. There were conflicting views as to whether the enclave could, or should, be defended. There were those, like Ad-

No Pushover

Fred O. Seibel/*Richmond Times-Dispatch*, 1948.

miral William D. Leahy, Truman's personal military adviser, who regarded the situation in Berlin as hopeless and America's ultimate withdrawal as unavoidable. And there were others, like Clay and Charles S. Murphy, who, while fully aware of Berlin's strategic vulnerability, thought that there were overriding political reasons for staying there. The final decision had to be made at the highest level, and Truman, characteristically, made a clear-cut decision and carried it through. Having reached the decision to stay in Berlin without the benefit of a unanimous recommendation, he went out of his way to reassure the doubters that this was the right decision. And he never wavered in his own conviction that this was the right decision. A number of distinct perceptual strands went into the making of this fundamental choice. They are recalled and elaborated upon in Truman's memoirs. First and foremost was the image of the Soviet Union as a threat to American security and world peace—a threat which could be countered effectively only from a position of strength. Among the things which, according to Truman's account, combined to convince him to seek reelection, "the threat being posed by Russian imperialist Communism" is placed at the top of the list. In 1948, he writes, there was no doubt in his mind about the course he had to take:

> The world was undergoing a major readjustment, with revolution stalking most of the "have-not" nations. Communism was making the most of this opportunity, thriving on misery as it always does. The course of freedom was being challenged again—this time from a new and powerful quarter—Soviet Russia.

> I had learnt from my negotiations with the intransigent Russian diplomats that there was only one way to avoid a third world war, and that was to lead from strength. We had to rearm ourselves and our allies and, at the same time, deal with the Russians in a manner they could never interpret as weakness.

> Within our own nation I had seen many well-meaning groups who campaigned for "peace at any price" while apologizing for the aggressive acts of the Russians as merely a reflection of Russian reaction to our own tough policy. Many respectable Americans espoused such ideas without realizing the danger to which they

were subjecting our national security and the freedoms for which we had fought so hard. . . .

I also felt, without undue ego, that this was no time for a new and inexperienced hand to take over the government.

Drawing on Experience

Truman prided himself on having the correct image of the Soviet Union because it was the product of experience, in contrast to the image held by Henry Wallace, which he depicted as the product of wishful thinking. Wallace had consistently maintained that Truman was too rough in dealing with the Soviets and that peace could be obtained with a more conciliatory approach. Truman disagreed: "I knew from personal experience that the Wallace dream of appeasement was futile and that, if allowed to materialize, it would be tragic. I had learnt that the Russians understood only force. Wallace did not think this was true, but he did not have the experience with the Soviets that had been mine."

Russian interference with Western access to Berlin fit in with the pattern of action which Truman had come to expect as a result of his experience. "The Berlin blockade," he asserts, "was a move to test our capacity and will to resist. This action and the previous attempts to take over Greece and Turkey were part of a Russian plan to probe for soft spots in the Western Allies' positions all around their own perimeter." He had no doubt at all about the real significance of the Russian action: "What the Russians were trying to do was to get us out of Berlin. At first they took the position that we never had a legal right to be in Berlin. Later they said that we had had the right but that we had forfeited it."

Deciding to Stay in Berlin

America's alleged legal rights of access to Berlin were the object of attention and comment by Truman. When finalizing the American commitment to remain in Berlin in the White House meeting on June 28, he remarked that, whatever the consequences, the essential decision was "that we were in Berlin by terms of an agreement and that the Russians had no right to get us out by either direct or indirect pressure." The significance of this statement lies in the fact that it was made to the President's advisers behind closed doors and not to the public. It supports the proposition that, in thinking through America's politico-strategic position, legal factors constituted one of the parameters and that these factors were not purely post-decision instruments of policy justification. But it also reveals a highly subjective interpretation of America's legal rights, which stemmed from an instinctive moralism and self-righteousness rather than from a careful study of the facts. In his memoirs, Truman again conveniently glosses over the fact that only America's air corridors to Berlin were secured in 1945 by written agreement, while access by land routes was not, and hence that, technically, the Soviet Union was not infringing America's legal rights. "It is my opinion," he writes, "that it would have made very little difference to the Russians whether or not there was an agreement in writing. What was at stake in Berlin was not a contest over legal rights, although our position was entirely sound in international law, but a struggle over Germany and, in a larger sense, over Europe."

The last sentence contains the central perceptual strand which led to the decision to stay in Berlin—namely, that the Soviet challenge was not confined to America's legal rights over Berlin, but extended to her basic commitment to check the march of communism in Europe. Truman repeatedly emphasized the magnitude and the insidious nature of the Soviet challenge: "In the face of our launching of the Marshall Plan, the Kremlin tried to mislead the people of Europe into believing that our interest and support would not extend beyond economic matters and that we would back away from any military risks." He realized, however, that the Kremlin was not riding the crest of a wave, but was desperately trying to score a victory after a long series of defeats: "The Russians were obviously determined to force us out of Berlin. They had suffered setbacks recently in Italy, in France, in Finland. Their strongest satellite, Yugoslavia, had suddenly developed a taste for independent action, and the European Recovery Program was beginning to succeed. The blockade of Berlin was international Communism's counterattack."

That this counterattack was launched in Berlin was considered doubly significant: first, because the city was of symbolic importance, and, second, because of American vulnerability there. As Truman put it: "The Kremlin had chosen perhaps the most sensitive objective in Europe—Berlin, the old capital of Germany, which was and is a symbol to the Germans. If we failed to maintain our position there, Communism would gain great strength among the Germans. Our position in Berlin was precarious. If we wished to remain there, we would have to make a show of strength. But there was always the risk that the Russian reaction might lead to war."

The risk of war weighed heavily on Truman and was one of the crucial considerations against the use of force to resolve the problem. "We had to face the possibility," he recalled, "that Russia might deliberately choose to make Berlin the pretext for war, but a more immediate danger was the risk that a trigger-happy Russian pilot or a hot-headed Communist tank commander might create an incident that could ignite the powder keg."

Initially, Truman may have hoped that the crisis would be resolved through negotiation. This, at any rate, is suggested by his description of the airlift as a temporary expedient to gain time. On June 26, he directed that Clay's improvised airlift be put on a full-scale organized basis and that every plane available to the European Command be pressed into service. "In this way," he recalls, "we hoped that we might be able to feed Berlin until the diplomatic deadlock could be broken."

Ordering the Airlift

But he did not take long to reach the conclusion that diplomacy did not offer a way out and that the U.S. must take action to stay in Berlin despite the risks of war inherent in such action. The gnawing doubts which afflicted his advisers did not affect his own basic predisposition to see the situation in plain black and white without any shades in-between. This predisposition led him to reach a decision instinctively and without any prolonged reflection and soul-searching. On June 28, only four days after the start of the blockade, at a meeting in the White House at which the specific question was raised as to whether or not the U.S. would stay in Berlin, "the President interrupted to say that there was no decision on that point, we were going to stay, period." Besides the domestic and international considerations, Truman's self-image as the leader of the Administration who must bear full responsibility and his innate preference for clear-cut choices affected the content of his decision and the style in which he enforced it. In his diary, Truman penned the following account of the meetings held on July 19:

> Have quite a day. See some politicos. A meeting with General Marshall and Jim Forrestal on Berlin and the Russian situation. Marshall states the facts and conditions with which we are faced. I made the decision ten days ago to *stay in Berlin*. Jim wants to hedge. . . . I insist we will stay in Berlin—come what may. Royall, Draper and Jim Forrestal come in later. I have to listen to a rehash of what I know already and reiterate my "Stay in Berlin" decision. I do not pass the buck, nor do I alibi out of any decision I make.

But while Truman did not pass the buck and assumed

full responsibility for staying in Berlin, domestic and foreign policy calculations made him reluctant to undertake measures which might escalate the crisis to the threshold of armed hostilities. It is for this reason that he ultimately rejected the idea of sending an armed convoy to break the blockade—an idea which appealed to his combative temperament—in favor of the more cautious policy of supplying Berlin with an airlift. Truman's caution stemmed in part from his image of the opponent's bargaining style. To him the Soviet Union appeared to be a shrewd and wily opponent, but also one capable of acting impetuously and even irrationally. Contrary to the view of his hard-line advisers, who believed that Moscow would not run any risks of World War III until ready for it, Truman believed that the crisis indicated that the Kremlin was willing to risk military incidents to test U.S. firmness and patience. Nor did he dismiss the possibility that Moscow was seeking a pretext for war. The reluctance to supply such a pretext and the fear of needlessly provoking the Soviets were important considerations in Truman's mind during the crisis. They served as a constraint on the means he would use to protect America's interests.

PRESIDENTS
and their
DECISIONS

CHAPTER

3

THE
KOREAN WAR

The Threat of Communism Led to Truman's Decision to Intervene in Korea

Burton I. Kaufman

In the following selection, Burton I. Kaufman details the political pressures that led to President Truman's decision to send troops to South Korea in June 1950. The greatest pressure was the public's fear that the Soviet Union was gaining the upper hand in the Cold War. In particular, notes Kaufman, the U.S. government was concerned that all of Southeast Asia would be controlled by the Communists if South Korea were to fall. There were also growing concerns about Communist subversion at home, due in part to Senator Joseph McCarthy's announcement that more than 200 State Department employees were Communists. According to Kaufman, Truman sent troops to Korea in part to deflate conservative charges that he was "soft" on communism. Kaufman is a professor of history and humanities at Virginia Polytechnic Institute and State University (Virginia Tech) in Blacksburg, Virginia, and the author of *The Korean War: Challenges in Crisis, Credibility, and Command.*

WHY DID THE TRUMAN ADMINISTRATION DECIDE ON military action in a part of the world that it had

Excerpted from *The Korean War: Challenges in Crisis, Credibility, and Command,* 2nd ed., by Burton I. Kaufman. Copyright © 1997, 1986, by The McGraw-Hill Companies, Inc. Reprinted by permission of The McGraw-Hill Companies, Inc.

just a few months earlier dismissed as having no military or strategic importance? What were the political pressures that Truman was under and what influences did they have on his final decision to commit ground forces to Korea? Did he have other choices, and why, during the days of decision, was each action that he took less than what was needed but his basic determination of what was necessary went unchallenged? Finally, why was the fateful decision regarding Formosa and Indochina made so quickly and with so little debate? . . .

A Unilateral Response

The reasons behind the American response to the attack are . . . complex, although in the final analysis, they can be reduced to one fundamental consideration. In the first place, bringing the invasion to the United Nations appeared the only reasonable course of action. The United States had earlier acted within the framework of the United Nations, and taking the matter to the Security Council was a way of serving notice to the world as to how seriously the United States viewed the fighting in Korea. It was also a way of achieving a collective response to the invasion, which seemed preferable to unilateral American action.

Yet almost from the time they first received news of the invasion, American officials both in South Korea and in Washington responded in a way that made a unilateral American response likely. Most important, they perceived the North Korean move across the border as a Soviet-sponsored and Soviet-controlled attack meant to test American resolve to resist Communist expansion that would have serious consequences throughout the Far East and Southeast Asia. As a State Department intelligence estimate put it, the elimination of South Korea would influence both Soviet and Chinese moves in Indochina, Formosa, Malaysia, and Burma.

In this regard, North Korea's invasion of South Korea

came at a time when the United States was already undertaking a major shift in its far eastern policy as a result of the loss of China to the Communists. Anticipating the Communist victory in China, Washington had decided by 1949 to resurrect Japan as a major power in East Asia, which would protect and promote the interests of the United States throughout the region. A politically stable and economically reconstructed Japan would play a central role in America's Pacific defense perimeter, as [Secretary of State Dean] Acheson had outlined before the National Press Club in January. It would also provide markets and be an engine of economic growth and accompanying political stability for the very nations of Southeast Asia it had sought to incorporate into its World War II "Greater East Asia Co-Prosperity Sphere." Conversely, the Asian hinterland would provide the raw materials, markets, and resources necessary for Japan's own economic growth and stability.

From a geopolitical standpoint alone, therefore, it was necessary to prevent communist domination of Korea, whose vital port of Pusan was separated from Japan by only about 100 miles. But Secretary of State Acheson also regarded South Korea as a "breadbasket" for Japan, which, before World War II, had imported about thirty percent of its food supply (mainly rice) from Korea and which, on the eve of the Korean War, still needed to import large quantities of rice as well as other food supplies and raw materials. In addition, the secretary expected Korea to become a major market for Japan as the Japanese went through the process of reindustrialization. In short, control of Korea by the Communists posed as much a threat to Japan and America's other Asian interests as domination of Korea by an unfriendly power threatened the Soviet Union's Asian interests.

Avoiding Damage to America's Prestige

In addition, a very real concern existed in Washington that the failure of the United States to take any action in Korea

Acheson's Influence

Secretary of State Dean Acheson was one of President Truman's most important advisers. In the following excerpt from his book Refighting the Last War: Command and Crisis in Korea 1950–1953, *D. Clayton James explains how Acheson was responsible for most of the initial decisions in the Korean War.*

Truman himself regarded the intervention of the United States in the Korean conflict as the "toughest decision" of his career, but, in truth, Secretary of State [Dean] Acheson was the actual initiator of most of the key early decisions. Truman was at his home in Independence, Missouri, when he heard of the outbreak of war along the 38th parallel, and Acheson rapidly made the initial basic decisions in Washington. When Truman got back to the nation's capital on June 26, he concurred in Acheson's prompt action to obtain the United Nations Security Council's resolution calling for a cease-fire in Korea and the withdrawal of the North Korean invaders from South Korea. Although he liked the strategic recommendations his secretary of state put before him, he realized they pointed toward quick involvement of American troops. Acheson also understood the consequences. "It looked as though we must steel ourselves for the use of force," he later said of the conclusion he had reached even before Truman's return. Acheson admitted that before

would cause significant damage to American prestige in Europe and the Middle East. Very much on the minds of America's leaders, including President Truman and Secretary of State Acheson, was the need to avoid another case of appeasement along the lines of the ill-fated and notorious Munich Conference of 1938, which they believed had nurtured Adolf Hitler's ambitions at world dominance.

Domestic considerations also weighed heavily on the Truman administration's decision to intervene in Korea.

he went to Blair House on the night of June 26 to confer with the President and other key executive advisers, his own mind "was pretty clear on where the course we were about to recommend would lead and why it was necessary that we follow the course."

In the next days of tense conferences between Truman and his top advisers, the President went along with virtually all the proposals put forth by Acheson, who, in turn, was framing the early strategic and diplomatic initiatives of the United States in the Korean War. Acheson, not Truman, was the most fervent proponent of committing American air, naval, and ground forces to the Korean action, and it was the secretary of state who was the instigator of the Security Council's resolution on June 27 calling upon member states to contribute men and materiel to the defense of South Korea. Moreover, Truman's bypassing of Congress was undertaken upon the persistent advice of Acheson. So strong was Acheson's influence on Truman that none of the foremost military officials who were involved in the Blair House sessions that final week of June, including boisterous Secretary of Defense Johnson and much-respected Chairman of the Joint Chiefs of Staff Omar Bradley, challenged the secretary of state's main ideas, even on military matters.

D. Clayton James, *Refighting the Last War: Command and Crisis in Korea 1950–1953*. New York: Free Press, 1993.

As the historian Stephen Pelz has remarked, Truman "was vulnerable to serious charges from his domestic critics if he did not intervene." If Korea fell to the Communists so soon after the fall of China, this might very well lead to a congressional investigation into the military reasons for the fall. Such an investigation would show that the administration had left the United States badly weakened militarily. A cutback in conventional forces as a result of budget restrictions, the lack of an adequate atomic deterrent to a Soviet attack in Europe or elsewhere, and inadequate war planning would be some of the charges made by administration critics and confirmed by a congressional investigation. The insufficiency of America's military aid to South Korea would be another charge.

Truman's own insecurity in foreign affairs; his frequent detachment and often episodic involvement in decision-making; his tendency to rely heavily on others he admired, such as Secretary of State Dean Acheson, for advice; his own strong anti-communism; and his inclination to react emotionally, spontaneously (and sometimes unwisely) against perceived injustices and personal affronts, all of which would become more apparent and instrumental as the war continued in Korea, must also be factored into any explanation of why the White House responded as it did to the North Korean invasion. For decision-making does not always follow in the orderly, rational, and deliberative manner that post-crisis analyses sometimes suggest. And there can be no doubt that Truman, who was ill-informed about Korea and caught completely off-guard by the North Korean attack, quickly came under great pressure to respond militarily.

A Climate of Fear and Crisis

Similarly, Truman had to contend with the general climate of fear and crisis that gripped the United States in the spring and early summer of 1950. At the time that North Korea invaded South Korea, the United States seemed to many Americans imperiled by the threat of Communism both at home and abroad. Events of the previous year hardly augured well for the future. First there had been the news in September 1949 that the Soviet Union had successfully tested an atomic bomb several years ahead of schedule. A month later Americans had learned that China had been "lost" to the Communists. The following January, Alger Hiss, a former State Department official who in testimony before a congressional committee had denied charges that he had been a Communist in the 1930s, was found guilty of perjury. At about the same time, Klaus Fuchs, a high-level atomic scientist, confessed in England to giving atomic secrets to the Soviet Union. And in February, Senator Joseph McCarthy of Wisconsin announced before a group of Republican women in Wheeling, West Virginia, that he had a list of 205 officials of the State Department who were members of, or loyal to, the Communist Party.

Taken together, these developments suggested to many Americans that the tide of the Cold War was running in favor of the Communists. More than that, they seemed to support charges of conspiracy even within Washington itself. Americans felt particularly betrayed by the "fall" of China, a country with which, it was widely believed, the United States had always had a special relationship. It mattered little that Chiang Kai-shek had been thoroughly corrupt or that his regime lacked popular support. For a large number of Americans, China could have been saved from communism had the administration been more resolute and forthcoming in its support of Chiang. A China lobby closely associated with the right wing of the Republican Party railed against the administration's Far East policy, attributing the Communist victory in China to the traitorous actions of diplomatic officials employed by Roosevelt and Truman.

Much of the bipartisanship that had characterized American foreign policy in recent years and been responsible for approval of the Truman Doctrine and the Marshall Plan vanished amid partisan wrangling over the China issue and the priority the administration gave to affairs in Europe. The China lobby increased its political strength in Washington, and Senator McCarthy became headline news as he continued to make charges of internal subversion and espionage. A new word, "McCarthyism," was introduced into the language to describe unsupported accusations of disloyalty and demagoguery. But for many Americans Mc-

Carthy's accusations offered convincing explanations of why China had been lost to the Communists and why the Soviet Union had developed a nuclear capability so fast.

Charges That the President Was "Soft" on Communism

The conspiratorial mentality that existed in America in 1950, however, was not limited to the anti-Communist hysteria and antics of Joseph McCarthy and those beholden to him. It was widespread and growing, and it intruded itself most forcibly in the national debate over the administration's far eastern policy. It was thus imperative for Truman to intervene in Korea, for the loss of that country so soon after the Communist victory in China would almost certainly have added to the storm of protest over the administration's Asian policy, raised additional accusations of internal subversion (which happened anyway), and, at the very least, furthered the already existing charges that the President was "soft" on communism.

In other words, the credibility of the administration's foreign policy was at issue in the Korean War, both abroad and at home, both among America's allies and its adversaries. In such a situation of crisis as seemed to face the United States in the summer of 1950, the President had to act forthrightly and unequivocally. Anything less would be an indication of weakness on his part, which the enemies of the United States and the foes of the administration could use to their benefits. Once Truman and his closest advisers accepted these basic assumptions—as they did almost immediately after receiving news of the fighting in Korea—there really seemed no course open to them other than the one they followed. . . .

A Deliberate Decision

Washington's decision to intervene in Korea, then, was made deliberately and in consideration of a Soviet response either in Korea or elsewhere. Its action in expanding aid to Indochina and the Philippines and neutralizing Formosa was also in large measure a product of this perception of a worldwide Communist threat. It is true that the course it followed, particularly its commitment of combat forces to Korea, was made easier by the lack of military action or even preparation for a military attack by Moscow or Beijing, either in Korea or some other danger spot. But irrespective of other considerations, the Truman administration felt it had no alternative except to prevent South Korea from falling to the Communists. In simplest terms, American credibility in the world and its own credibility at home were at issue.

Throughout most of the period after World War II, the United States had attempted a policy of disengagement from Korea and all the rest of the Asian mainland. But the imperatives of the Cold War, the conviction that the world was in peril, that the tide of events was not going well for the United States, and that in the global confrontation with the Soviet Union America had to support any country and any regime threatened by communism, led the United States by 1950 into military involvement in a part of the world few Americans knew anything about and in a country that only a short time earlier had been deemed to be outside America's defense perimeter.

Truman Made Several Poor Decisions During the Korean War

Donald Johnston

President Truman's strategy during the Korean War was flawed for several reasons, argues Korean War veteran Donald Johnston in the following selection. Johnston criticizes the president's decision to send American troops to South Korea without officially declaring war. The Truman administration had called it a "police action," rather than a war, so the president would not need to receive congressional approval. He also asserts that Truman's strategy of maintaining the status quo in South Korea—instead of seeking victory—was a mistake because it placed soldiers in a purposeless war. Johnston concludes that the mistakes of the Korean War have been repeated in Vietnam and elsewhere, ultimately changing the role of the American military and the nature of war.

THE KOREAN WAR STARTED JUNE 25, 1950, WITH THE INvasion of South Korea by the North Korean army. The United States entered the fray June 30, 1950, joining the Republic of Korea army in its defense of South Korea.

A number of other countries contributed military personnel, but they represented less than 10 percent of the total. On July 7, 1950, General Douglas MacArthur was ap-

Excerpted from "Lessons from Korea," by Donald Johnston, *American Legion Magazine,* September 2000. Reprinted with permission.

pointed by President Truman as the Supreme Commander of the U.N. forces in Korea.

Why the war in Korea? To answer that, one has to look back to World War II. The war ended with the American and Soviet armies racing toward each other. Where they stopped would become a new dividing line between communism and freedom.

While post-war treaties called on the Soviets to hold free and open elections in their occupied lands, Soviet leader Joseph Stalin failed to abide by his promises. Just as Germany was cut in half, so was Korea divided between a Soviet zone and American zone, the Soviet Union controlling the northern portion of the peninsula.

Truman became president after Franklin D. Roosevelt's death in April 1945. Gen. George Marshall, then-secretary of state, and Dean Acheson, undersecretary of state, quickly planned a Western-oriented government for South Korea in which that country would become a trade partner with Japan (occupied by the United States). This would create a powerhouse of capitalism in Asia that hopefully would prove to be a more dynamic economic force than communism. In theory, this partially capitalistic Asia would then spread to become an all-capitalistic Asia with Japan, organized by the United States, at its center.

To thwart such a plan, Stalin plotted the invasion and takeover of South Korea, which triggered America's response.

An Undeclared War

In an effort to make the United States' move appear sanctioned by the rest of the world, Truman had taken the issue not to Congress, as required by the Constitution, but to the U.N. Security Council, which unanimously approved the motion. (The Soviet Union was staging a protest over another matter and had earlier walked out of the Security Council. Its delegation was not present to use its veto power.)

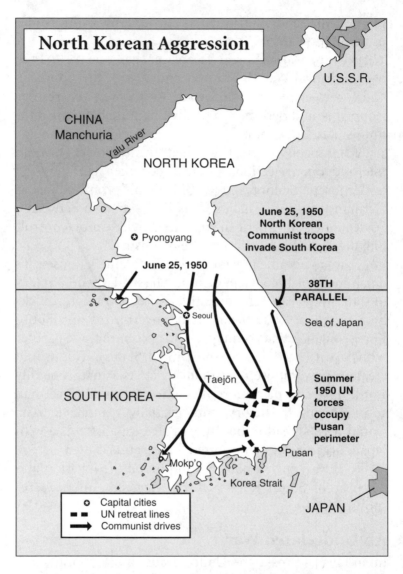

North Korean Aggression

U.S.S.R.

CHINA
Manchuria

Yalu River

NORTH KOREA

June 25, 1950
North Korean
Communist troops
invade South Korea

○ Pyongyang

June 25, 1950

38TH
PARALLEL

✪ Seoul

Sea of Japan

Taejŏn

Summer
1950 UN
forces
occupy
Pusan
perimeter

SOUTH KOREA

Mokp'○

Pusan

Korea Strait

JAPAN

○ Capital cities
■ ■ ■ UN retreat lines
➤ Communist drives

Truman and his supporters used semantics to defend the decision not to ask for a declaration of war.

If the word "war" was not employed, the Truman administration tacitly argued, a president could send troops anywhere in the world for any purpose. Korea would be a "police action," the first of many such undeclared wars. And the constitutional system would be irrevocably altered.

Initially, U.N. forces were thrown back in Korea. However, on Sept. 15, 1950, Operation CHROMITE, MacArthur's plan to land behind enemy lines at Inchon, crushed the North Korean forces in a pincer movement between the U.N. troops in the south and the invading U.N. troops to the north.

By November 1950, the North Korean army had been obliterated, and the war was basically over—all in just five months. There was even talk of the troops returning home by the Christmas holidays.

But two decisions would make that impossible. The first was made in Washington. "I have ordered the 7th Fleet to prevent any attack on Formosa," Truman said two days after the invasion of South Korea. "As a corollary of this action, I am calling upon the Chinese government on Formosa (Taiwan) to cease all air and sea operations against the mainland. The 7th Fleet will see that this is done."

That decision enabled China to move the major portion of its military might away from its southeastern coast, since there was no fear that the forces under Chiang Kai-shek would make incursions from Formosa.

The other decision was made in Beijing. No longer concerned by attack from the nationalists on Formosa, the Chinese decided to intervene in Korea. As U.N. forces mopped up, hundreds of thousands of communist soldiers secretly infiltrated North Korea, moving under the cover of night and hiding in the valleys and caves during the day to avoid detection by U.N. aerial reconnaissance.

Maj. Gen. Charles Willoughby, intelligence officer for MacArthur, had estimated this force to be only 60,000 to 70,000. However, Maj. Gen. Edward Almond estimated 300,000 Chinese infiltrators and feared the Chinese were setting a trap for U.N. forces.

Regrettably, Gen. Almond's estimate was far more accurate. The 300,000 Chinese turned out to be Gen. Lin

Piao's 4th Field Army and Gen. Chen Yi's 3rd, though China always referred to the troops as "volunteers." MacArthur and Willoughby's miscalculation would become a rallying point for MacArthur's detractors. When the Communist Chinese forces came out of hiding from the remote mountain ravines in North Korea to attack U.N. forces Nov. 25, 1950, this signaled the start of a new war: the Chinese army against the U.N. forces.

As the Chinese crossed the Yalu River, the border between China and North Korea, they received protection from an unexpected source: Washington. MacArthur had ordered the bridges on the Yalu River to be destroyed by the U.S. Air Force to stop the invasion of Chinese troops, but he was shocked to find his orders were countermanded by Gen. George C. Marshall, secretary of defense. Truman and Marshall feared that escalation in Korea

A Ridiculous Stalemate

President Truman's strategy in Korea was widely questioned by Republican congressmen. One of the most outspoken critics was Ohio senator Robert A. Taft. In the following excerpt from a speech he gave in front of the Senate, Taft questions the president's decision to fight a stalemate war.

Policy No. 2 [was] proposed by the President last night. It is a Maginot-line policy. We are to continue to conduct a war with our hands tied behind our backs. We are to refuse all assistance from the Chinese Nationalists. It is like a football game in which our team, when it reaches the 50-yard line, is always instructed to kick. Our team can never score, and sooner or later somebody on the other side will catch the ball and make a touchdown. As I read the President's speech, he suggests that if we don't notice that the Chinese are there in Korea, after a while they will go away. His hopes and China would force America to shift forces from Germany to Asia, thus leaving a weakened defense in Europe against possible moves by Stalin. After the Chinese intervention, there was also fear that Korea would touch off a third world war.

"I realized for the first time that I had actually been denied the use of my full military power to safeguard the lives of my soldiers and the safety of my army," MacArthur would later state. "To me, it clearly foreshadowed a future tragic situation in Korea."

Oddly, MacArthur's feelings were shared by his adversary: "I never would have made the attack and risked my men and my military reputation if I had not been assured that Washington would restrain General MacArthur from taking adequate retaliatory measures against my lines of supply and communication," General Piao recounted.

---

are almost pitiful. If we inflict sufficient casualties, he says, this "may discourage the Chinese Communists from continuing their attack." If they see the world arming "this may discourage the Communist rulers from continuing the war in Korea." If they realize they cannot defeat us in Korea (except to the extent they have already done so) "then they may recognize the folly of continuing their aggression. A peaceful settlement may then be possible." This certainly proposes a stalemate war. It makes a joke of the United Nations ban against aggression, and encourages aggression elsewhere. The President himself points out that back in China there "stand additional millions of Chinese soldiers." They will have lost nothing except a few men, and manpower in China is cheap. It is ridiculous to say that we are preventing either aggression or world war III by this stalemate war.

Robert A. Taft, remarks before the U.S. Senate, April 13, 1951.

Any possibility of victory in 1950 had been successfully negated.

MacArthur was fighting to win in Korea. Truman wanted to maintain the status quo. This was an unprecedented conflict of attitudes regarding the definition of war. Should the objective be MacArthur's "no substitute for victory" or a more limited, politically sensitive policy?

The answer remains in dispute even today, but after three years of limited war and stalled negotiations, one thing is clear: Truman's war strategy created untenable situations for the men who fought and died in Korea.

The differences between MacArthur and Truman would prove too deep to smooth over, and on April 11, 1951, MacArthur was replaced by Lt. Gen. Matthew Ridgway as Supreme Commander.

Armistice talks began in July 1951. By Oct. 28, agreement on a line of the demarcation between North and South Korea was determined. On Nov. 12, Ridgway ordered Lt. Gen. James Van Fleet, commander of the 8th Army, to halt offensive operations and commence active defense of the U.N. front. For the first time in U.S. history, our armed forces were deliberately practicing stalemate while the negotiators floundered at Panmunjom.

U.N. forces had been ordered to establish a holding position along the agreed-upon truce line. With the exception of extremely bloody battles such as the capture of the Korean hill, Old Baldy, by the 45th Infantry Division in June 1952, the war became a stalemate. It was punctuated by nightly firefights and patrols to reconnoiter enemy positions for information.

The question heard with the greatest frequency was simply, "Why are we here?" There seemed no purpose to this static war—other than to kill and wait to be killed.

The treaty talks that had started in July 1951 dragged on until President Eisenhower (sworn into office in January 1953) removed the 7th Fleet blockade of Formosa and gave notice to the Chinese government that the United States was going to attack bases in China and might use the atomic bomb. Two weeks later, July 27, 1953, the treaty was signed. No matter what the exigencies of the situation and arguments that can be made for committing U.S. citizen-soldiers to the war in Korea, one compelling argument against the decision surfaces. When committing the lives of citizens of a free country to war, their lives should not be sacrificed upon the altar of world politics—a war of attrition in which their lives are snuffed out as they wait for the politicians to try to negotiate terms with an enemy that is satisfied to stall until their antagonists simply give up.

In the wake of this "police action," Gen. Mark W. Clark, who succeeded Ridgway as Supreme Commander of the United Nations forces May 7, 1952, said, "It was beyond my comprehension that we would countenance a situation in which Chinese soldiers killed American youth in organized, formal warfare, and yet we would fail to use all the power at our command to protect those Americans."

Approximately 34,000 U.S. military personnel died in Korea, with an astonishing number of nearly 107,000 wounded and missing. Total U.N. losses, including ROK army units, were more than 995,000. Total Chinese losses were 900,000, while North Korean losses were 520,000. Altogether, the communists lost 1,420,000.

Many surviving personnel came home bitter, emotionally altered and with minimal trust in their government. Marine Cpl. Frank Bifulk's sentiments were shared by many other Korean veterans: "Truman really slapped us in the face," Bifulk concluded in 1950. "He called Korea a police action. Here we were in Korea fighting and dying, and our president says that. Some thanks."

The Aftermath of the Korean War
Aside from such human and emotional costs of the war, there were long-term political consequences.

Executive powers were markedly expanded. The boldest assumption of power was the assigning of U.S. troops to military action in Korea without prior congressional consent. With the semantic twist of calling the Korean War a "police action" instead of what it was—a war—future presidents would send troops anywhere in the world for any purpose without approval, using the Korean precedent as their justification.

Vietnam, Kosovo, Bosnia, a number of mini-wars and even the Gulf War indicate that Truman's methods have been repeatedly embraced by his successors.

In the wake of the Truman-MacArthur standoff, the tradition that obliged presidents to defer to field commanders during times of war came to an end. Truman-style micromanagement has reared its head in nearly every conflict since.

Finally, the role of the U.S. military was changed. Formerly, its function was to defend the United States and its citizens from foreign danger. In Korea, that role was expanded to include peacekeeping for the United Nations. What Truman did in this regard in Korea was imitated by other presidents in Lebanon, the Persian Gulf, Somalia, Bosnia and scores of other U.N. missions.

MacArthur concluded that Truman's decision to prevent the bombing of the bridges between Korea and China "foreshadowed a future tragic situation in Korea." In the same manner, Korea itself foreshadowed the future tragedy of undeclared wars.

The Truman-MacArthur Controversy Exemplifies Differing Views on the Korean War

James L. Stokesbury

In the following essay, James L. Stokesbury describes how President Truman fired Douglas MacArthur after the general challenged American policy in Korea. One key episode was MacArthur's criticism of a December 1950 directive that changed the mission of the Korean War, from an earlier goal to "restore international peace and security" to a new plan to defend the positions that the American and United Nations troops held in Korea. The policy change was a response to Communist China's entry into the conflict in November: MacArthur wanted to carry the war to the Chinese mainland, while Truman believed that doing so might lead to a full-scale war with the Soviet Union.

The conflict between the two men came to a head in March 1951. According to Stokesbury, MacArthur's offer that month to begin negotiations to end the war showed how the general refused to acknowledge Truman's policies and made his dismissal inevitable. MacArthur's disagreements with Truman were further publicized when the general sent a letter to Congressman Joseph W. Martin Jr., declaring that there was "no substitute for victory"; Martin read the letter in front of the House of Representatives, prompting Truman to dismiss MacArthur. Stokesbury is a historian whose books include *A Short History of World*

War II and *A Short History of the Korean War,* from which this selection has been excerpted.

████████████

THE FAMOUS TRUMAN-MACARTHUR CONTROVERSY IS REally misnamed. It was not so much a matter between the general and the President, though in the course of it they managed to work up a substantial dislike for each other; nor was it, in its essentials, too much of a controversy, even if it seemed to be a matter of great import at the time. The issue was not, for example, civilian control of the military, which was never seriously questioned. Such a problem would have been clear-cut black and white. MacArthur's relief, like almost everything else in the Korean War, or the whole era, was a matter of grays, of blurred nuances and shadowy distinctions.

MacArthur's Lack of Support for American Policy

The feeling had long been growing in Washington, among the Joint Chiefs of Staff, the State Department, and the President and his advisers, that General MacArthur neither was in sympathy with nor entirely understood the evolution of national policy toward the rest of the world. Part of the difficulty arose, certainly, from the fact that the government was not sure itself exactly what its policy was. The United States had decided to rebuild the free world and to resist the spread of Communism, but by what means and to what extent were uncertain. There were a few hard points: Europe was more important than Asia; the United States did not want to fight a third world war; the United States, under present circumstances, *could* not fight a third world war. But beyond these, it was a matter of responding to crises as they arose, trying to deal with urgent matters on a day-to-day basis, and often trying to make one resource answer two or three different needs.

For example, the war in Korea impeded the military buildup of United States forces in Europe; enlarging the Republic of Korea Army meant slowing the rearmament not only of America's European allies but even of the United States Army itself. So it went; the government, no matter how hard it tried to juggle resources, was still robbing Peter to pay Paul.

Korea was therefore seen as a very limited commitment, but the trouble with it was that it refused to stay within the limits Washington would have preferred. Indeed, Korea was a classic example of Clausewitz's dictum about force generating more force. North Korea's aggression led to the United Nations' intervention; the United Nations' intervention led in turn to Communist China's intervention; and, theoretically, so on and so on. The United States, however, did not now wish to pursue the "and so on"; it wished to end the war, not to fight World War III over a piece of Asian real estate that in itself was of only slight interest to the rest of the world.

As a result of these considerations, which of course are presented here in a vastly simplified form, the government sent General MacArthur, in his role as Commander in Chief Far East, a new directive on December 29, 1950. This new statement changed his primary mission in Korea; from the earlier "restore international peace and security" to "defend in successive positions . . . inflicting such damage to hostile forces in Korea as is possible, subject to the primary consideration of the safety of your troops." The directive then continued on to talk of the possibility of withdrawal from the peninsula. MacArthur responded to this by suggesting that since Red China had now entered the war, it ought to be carried to the Chinese mainland, possibly by blockade of the coast, air and naval bombardment, or the use of Chinese Nationalist forces, either in Korea or on the mainland itself. He concluded by challenging the whole policy of the government to avoid major Asian commitments while building up strength in Europe.

MacArthur Takes Action

This was all old stuff, for MacArthur had suggested use of the Chinese Nationalists, and direct action against China, before, and been rejected; but that was before Red China had intervened in Korea. Now he was trying it again. It must be noted here, parenthetically, that the issue of Chiang Kai-shek and the Nationalists kept intruding on the Korean problem. The Truman administration consistently tried to soft-pedal the Nationalist question, while General MacArthur, and the more aggressive elements in Washington, and the Republican opposition, equally often demanded or threatened Nationalist action against Communist China; there was a desire, in the phrase of the day, to "unleash the Nationalists." As a policy alternative, this would have been roughly equivalent to urging a mouse to attack a tiger, but it was a matter that bedeviled the whole period.

The real problem, of course, was not the Chinese Nationalists; it was rather the almost unique position occupied by MacArthur on the American scene. Officially he was but the military commander in the Far East; in fact he was far more than that. As an active soldier for close to half a century, he was far senior to his ostensible superiors in the Pentagon, and they treated him with a deference he really should not have had. This was especially true in the aftermath of Inchon, when he had been right and everyone else was wrong. But he also typified—and this was what the "controversy" was actually all about—the dilemma, indeed the impossibility, of drawing a clear line between what was "military" and what was "political" in the modern world, and what kind of advice, loyalty, acquiescence, obedience, or opposition the soldier owes to his political masters.

Two days after MacArthur received his new directive,

the Chinese attacked across the 38th parallel, then Seoul fell, and prospects in Korea looked dim indeed. But Eighth Army and the Republic of Korea (ROK) forces rallied, the situation stabilized, and the United Nations recovered the initiative. President Truman thought the time had come for a negotiated settlement. China had shown that it would not permit the Democratic People's Republic of (North) Korea to be destroyed, and the United States and the United Nations had now shown, twice, that they would not permit the Republic of (South) Korea to be destroyed. The short-lived myth of Chinese battlefield invincibility was being shattered by Ridgway's advances, and as the UN forces got back to the parallel, an obvious equilibrium was reached. Truman therefore prepared an announcement that the United Nations would welcome negotiations. Earlier UN attempts to move in this direction had been spurned by China, but that was before the battlefield defeats of February. While Truman's announcement was being cleared with the other governments supporting the Korean action, and MacArthur informed of its imminent release, the general took matters into his own hands.

On March 24, 1951, he issued a public statement. In it he pointed out that Red China was vastly overrated as a military power, and that if the United Nations chose to extend the war to their homeland, the Chinese would precipitately collapse. Then he offered to open negotiations to end the war. His statement totally eclipsed any Truman might have made, and was couched in an arrogant tone that made a positive response to it unthinkable.

President Truman was furious. He had already, on December 6, ordered that any such public pronouncements had to be cleared with Washington, and now here was the Great Pooh-Bah undercutting the government's carefully constructed plans. MacArthur blithely responded to Washington's complaints that he thought he was acting within the bounds of his authority.

A Dismissal and Return to Home

He was, however, already on the way out. For on March 20, four days before his famous public statement, he had written a letter to Congressman Joseph W. Martin, Jr. Mr. Martin happened to be the Republican minority leader in the House of Representatives, and he happened to be one of the advocates of "unleashing" Nationalist China. In his letter, MacArthur agreed fully with Mr. Martin's ideas, deplored the priority accorded Europe, announced that "we must win" in Asia, and concluded, "There is no substitute for victory." On April 5, Mr. Martin stood up on the floor of the House of Representatives and read General MacArthur's letter into the *Congressional Record*.

That did it. It took a few days for the Joint Chiefs, the Secretaries of State and Defense, and assorted other advisers to meet with the President and round it all off, but there was no question after April 5; MacArthur had to go.

The manner of his going was singularly unfortunate. He was to be relieved of command April 12, and since Secretary of the Army Frank Pace was touring the Far East Command at that time, the government's intention was to have Pace relieve him in a personal interview. But Pace was isolated by a communications breakdown in Korea, and the news of the impending blow got out to the reporters. Washington therefore decided to wire direct to Far East Command in Tokyo. The commercial wire services beat the Army's communications network. On April 11 the MacArthurs were hosting a luncheon at the U.S. Embassy when the general's aide, Col. Sidney Huff, heard the news on a Japanese radio station. He interrupted the meal to whisper to Mrs. MacArthur, who then whispered to her husband.

MacArthur took it in his stride, finished hosting the meal, and immediately began making preparations to give up his command and return to the United States.

His successor was General Matthew Ridgway, at the

moment up on the front lines in Korea showing Secretary Pace around. Neither of them knew anything about it for some time, but Ridgway was soon ensconced in Tokyo, and Gen. James A. Van Fleet took over Eighth Army.

MacArthur returned home to a hero's welcome in the States. His relief was a *cause célèbre*. He was lionized, but so was Truman; he was vilified, but so was Truman; some unions were for him, some were for Truman. State legislatures and universities debated the pros and cons, commending or condemning one side or the other. There was a parade in Honolulu, another in San Francisco, one in Washington, one in New York. In his most famous appearance, MacArthur spoke before Congress, defending his ideas, in fact repeating many of them, and he closed with the lines of the old army ballad, "Old soldiers never die; they just fade away."

He of course did not quite fade away, at least not for a while. There were books, there were public appearances, there were meetings. MacArthur was the man of the hour. There were several records released of the old soldier ballad, which at least had the virtue of being a pretty good song. Of MacArthur's speech before Congress, one listener, a congressman, thought it was the "voice of God." Truman, privately, fortunately not publicly, thought it was "a bunch of bullshit." In fact it was a terrific speech, though like many such, it did not say a great deal.

There was inevitably a Congressional hearing, in the Senate, and it went on interminably, from early May until August. By then almost everyone had had his innings—the transcript ran to 2 million words—and this had the effect such proceedings regularly do; it confused and obfuscated the issues, and eventually bored everyone. After that, MacArthur could truly fade away.

The war went on.

Truman Was Partially Vindicated in His Decision to Dismiss MacArthur

Harry J. Middleton

In the following essay, Harry J. Middleton writes that President Truman won only a partial victory in his battle against General Douglas MacArthur. According to Middleton, although Truman had the right to fire MacArthur, the method in which he did so was graceless. MacArthur won the immediate battle for public opinion, as millions greeted him when, following his return from Korea, he visited cities throughout America. Despite the initial outpouring for the general, who was also given the opportunity to speak before both houses of Congress, it was ultimately Truman's foreign policies in Korea that prevailed. Middleton is the author of *The Compact History of the Korean War* and the former director of the Lyndon Baines Johnson Library and Museum.

[O F HIS DECISION TO DISMISS GENERAL DOUGLAS MAC-Arthur, Truman said,] "If there is one basic element in our Constitution, it is civilian control of the military. . . . This was the principle that General MacArthur threatened" by showing "that he was unwilling to accept the policies of the Administration . . . confusing our allies as to the true course of our policies" and "in fact . . . setting his policy against the President's." Truman said he did not believe MacArthur "purposefully" set out to challenge civilian supremacy, "but the result of his behavior was that this fundamental principle of free government was in danger."

For Truman, "the time had come to draw the line." If he had not, with so vital a principle at stake, "I myself would be violating my oath to uphold and defend the Constitution."

[Secretary of State] Dean Acheson had told Truman, "If you relieve MacArthur, you will have the biggest fight of your Administration," and there could be little question but that that was what was shaping up when the dismissal became known. Cries for impeachment rang out in the Congress, and in at least one city the President was burned in effigy. In the main, the clamor centered on the thesis that the firing of MacArthur was an appeasement of, and a victory for, Communism. Even at its most violent and hysterical, the criticism focused thus on the President's judgment; there was little question, and none at all from any responsible group, including the military, about his *right* to take the action he had—in itself a testament to the strength of that principle of civilian supremacy which Truman had feared was in jeopardy. And hidden in the tumult, of course, their voices lost in its din, were all the many thousands who supported strongly what the President had done, or at least believed he had been left no choice.

A Graceless Firing

From no quarter, however, except perhaps that housing the most virulent MacArthur-haters, was there sympathy for the *manner* in which the President had taken his action: at one o'clock on the morning of April 11, 1951, he held a press conference where reporters were handed an announcement stating that because MacArthur "is unable to give his whole-hearted support to the policies of the United

States Government and of the United Nations in matters pertaining to his official duties ... I have decided that I must make a change of command in the Far East. I have, therefore, relieved General MacArthur of his commands ..." The actual relief order was dispatched to MacArthur at the same time, but because of delays in transmission, the news reached Tokyo ahead of the order.

Truman explained the circumstances this way: although he had already made up his mind to dismiss MacArthur, he wanted to get the views of his advisers. The day after Representative Joseph W. Martin produced his explosive letter, the President met with the Secretaries of State and Defense, General Bradley and Averell Harriman, and without revealing that he had made his decision, asked them to give him their recommendations [On March 20, 1951, MacArthur wrote a letter to Martin that detailed his

General Douglas MacArthur received grand support from the American public when he returned to the United States after being stripped of his title by Truman.

views on American foreign policy]. By April 9 he had from Bradley the unanimous conviction of the Joint Chiefs of Staff, concurred in by Marshall, that for "purely military considerations" alone, MacArthur should be relieved; the agreement of Acheson, who had long been worried that the Far East Commander would exercise his authority "in the direction of enlarging rather than confining the conflict" but who foresaw the domestic wars ahead; and Harriman's opinion that, in Truman's words, "I should have fired MacArthur two years ago." Thus solidly backed up, Truman revealed his decision. The orders stripping MacArthur were drafted. Truman signed them, and they were sent through State Department channels to the Embassy in Korea, where Secretary of the Army Frank Pace was on an inspection trip, along with instructions for Pace to take them over to Tokyo and deliver them personally to MacArthur. However, transmission difficulties again, and the fact that Pace was touring the front with Ridgway, delayed his getting them, and the next night—April 10— Truman decided he had to speed things up when he learned that a newspaper had uncovered the story and planned to run it the next morning. Truman never explained why this news leak should necessitate such an extraordinary handling of the situation, but the most likely reason was that he feared a premature report of the impending action would give MacArthur supporters in Congress an opportunity to rally a massive effort to block the President's move.

Whatever the reason, the effect was singularly rude and graceless. The word came to Tokyo Headquarters via a radio newscast heard by one of the general's aides while the MacArthurs were having lunch. "Never in history," MacArthur said later, had a more "drastic method" been employed to relieve a commander. "No office boy, no charwoman, no servant of any sort would have been dismissed with such callous disregard for the ordinary decencies."

An Outpouring of Support

The American people made it up to him, for no hero before him ever received such an extravagant welcome as was his when he returned to the United States for the first time in fifteen years. In Honolulu and San Francisco and New York and twenty cities after them, they stood along his routes of travel in the millions and cheered him to the skies; and they were only the privileged guard, cheering too for the many millions more across the land who belonged in the acclaiming crowds.

It was a memorable occasion in the nation's life, unique in its experience, and strangely a part of the disturbed and confused mood of the time, with all its contradictions. For this was the kind of welcome reserved for conquerors, and although MacArthur had many conquests to his credit, stretching back through World War II, whose rewards he had not been home to claim, his last great campaign had ended in defeat; and crowds are notoriously fast forgetters of earlier victories obscured by later failure. What, then, were they cheering? The victor he might have been? The battles he might have won . . . and the plan for victory he still carried in his mind?

That this was at the central core of that tremendous demonstration there could be no doubt, for the general's supporters were "legion," as Representative Martin had told him. But this was not all of it. The chorus of those hoarse hurrahs was never interpreted as a call to broaden the Korean War; the cheers were never negotiable into the kind of endorsement which can force new policy and—had that happened now—might have given the MacArthur mission a historic significance as unrivaled as was his welcome home.

The outpouring was heard, however, as a cry of protest; for Chong-chon and the long march down from Hagaru had changed forever the once near-unanimous endorsement of U.S. involvement. Disenchantment would grow steadily from now on. And the final anomaly of the MacArthur saga was that the leader who saw Korea as history's challenge to the West should become the symbol of defiance for those who came to see it only as a squalid war which we had no business fighting in the first place.

He was invited to address a Joint Session of Congress, and this too is an image permanently stamped on the memory of midcentury America—the aging but erect and proud figure telling the nation's lawmakers, and beyond them the nation itself: "I address you with neither rancor nor bitterness in the fading twilight of life but with one purpose in mind—to serve my country." He articulated the program which he felt "military necessity . . . made mandatory." (In one significant detail it was different from that which he had proposed to Washington in December: he did not talk now of employment of Chiang Kai-shek's troops, but of "removal of restrictions" on them "with logistical support to contribute to their effective operations against the common enemy.")

The heart of his message was an eloquent statement of his convictions:

> Efforts have been made to distort my position. It has been said that I was in effect a warmonger. Nothing could be further from the truth. I know war as few other men now living know it, and nothing to me is more revolting. . . . But once war is forced upon us, there is no other alternative than to apply every available means to bring it to a swift end. War's very object is victory—not prolonged indecision. In war, indeed, there can be no substitute for victory.

> There are some who for varying reasons would appease Red China. They are blind to history's clear lesson. For history teaches with unmistakable emphasis that appeasement but begets new and bloodier war. . . . Why, my

Outrage Toward Truman

President Truman's decision to dismiss General MacArthur sparked anger throughout America. In the following excerpt from his essay "The Korean War and American Society," John Edward Wiltz offers several examples of this animosity.

Americans who remember 1951 are not apt to forget the popular response to the dismissal orders. From Maine to California came thunderous expressions of outrage that Truman had sacked the imperious architect of the Allied victory in the Southwest Pacific during World War II and the bearer of democracy to conquered Japan. Referring to the president, whose public approval rating recently had slipped to 28 percent, Senator McCarthy said, "The son of a bitch ought to be impeached." Many other Americans agreed. *Life* magazine published a picture of a grinning Senator Richard M. Nixon holding a batch of telegrams urging

soldiers asked of me, surrender military advantages to an enemy in the field? I could not answer. Some may say to avoid spread of the conflict into an all-out war with China; others, to avoid Soviet intervention. Neither explanation seems valid. For China is already engaging with the maximum power it can commit and the Soviet will not necessarily mesh its actions with our moves. . . .

The dramatic farewell alone would have ensured the speech's enduring position in the nation's memory:

I am closing my fifty-two years of military service. When I joined the Army even before the turn of the century, it was the fulfillment of all my boyish hopes and dreams. The world has turned over many times since I took the oath on the Plain at West Point, and the hopes and dreams have long since vanished. But I still remember

Truman's impeachment; exuded Nixon, "It's the largest spontaneous reaction I've ever seen." Students in California hung the president in effigy; a woman in Maryland sent a telegram to the White House calling Truman a witling—after Western Union refused to transmit the word *moron;* and in Los Angeles a man told a television reporter that "the country would not be in this shape if Harry Truman were alive." (The same man then told the reporter that he was going out for a "Truman beer." "What kind of beer is that?" the reporter asked. "Just like any other kind," the man replied, "except it hasn't got a head.") When the Gallup organization sought a measure of the public's opinion of the MacArthur dismissal, it found that only 25 percent of those interviewed approved of the president's actions.

John Edward Wiltz, "The Korean War and American Society." From Francis H. Heller, ed., *The Korean War: A 25-Year Perspective,* 1977.

the refrain of one of the most popular barrack ballads of that day which proclaimed most proudly that—

"Old soldiers never die, they just fade away."

And like the old soldier of that ballad, I now close my military career and just fade away—an old soldier who tried to do his duty as God gave him the light to see that duty. Good-by.

The Effects of the MacArthur Hearings

Neither MacArthur nor Truman had a particularly high regard for the hearings which soon followed, conducted by the Combined Senate Committees on Armed Forces and Foreign Relations, to inquire into the military situation in the Far East and the circumstances of MacArthur's dismissal—MacArthur because "the Committee soon divided along partisan lines and its final report was of little value," and Truman because "the Committee Republicans (with few exceptions) made this an occasion to spread on the record almost every detail of our strategic planning."

Both lost something as a result of those hearings.

MacArthur was the immediate loser. For three days his position in all its ramifications was laid open to public view and then for a month rebutted by Administration spokesmen, including the members of the Joint Chiefs of Staff. When it was all over, MacArthur had not lost any of his dedicated followers, but neither had he made any converts; and there were many who had been only spectators, seeing the issues dimly but applauding MacArthur as the hero in a gripping drama of conflict, who nonetheless— when the drama turned to the courtroom and all the evidence was in—reluctantly gave their decision to the Administration.

History has yet to give its final verdict on the validity of MacArthur's position. He himself would live to see the power of Red China grow to frightening size, and to record in his autobiography the sobering words of a congressman who had once opposed him: ". . . Someday we will have to fight Red China on her terms at a time of her choosing. She will have atomic power backed by the entire Eurasian land mass. This issue could have been resolved forever in our favor in 1951 had those of us in Washington had the foresight to give MacArthur the green light in Asia. . . . MacArthur was right and many of us here in Washington, in London, and in the United Nations were wrong. . . ."

But the most telling point against MacArthur emerging from the mass of testimony in the Senate hearings was that the combined weight of constitutional authority, including the military leaders who were obliged to regard the nation's capabilities from a global view, believed that an enlargement of the war in Korea, along the lines MacArthur called for, would subject the United States to a major war in Asia which it could not hope to wage, and win, if it was simultaneously to deter war in Europe.

MacArthur himself in those hearings took on the cast of an evangelist of a holy cause; Truman and his Joint Chiefs the cast of pragmatists who believed in holiness up to a point but thereafter were concerned with safety. And while the sympathies and sometimes the passions of the Americans of the twentieth century have gone to the evangelists, they have followed the pragmatists. Despite the misgivings of the British and the other Allies whose influence was so heavily felt in Washington, MacArthur told the Senate investigators, Korea was the testing ground where the United States would have its final chance to defeat the dark powers of Communism. "Alone?" he was asked. And the General answered:

"Alone, if necessary. If the other nations of the world haven't got enough sense to see where appeasement leads after the appeasement which led to the Second World War in Europe, if they can't see exactly the road that they are following in Asia, why then, we had better protect ourselves and go it alone."

It took a dedicated believer to follow him after that, in the new age of collective security.

A Partial Victory for Truman

Harry Truman was the victor: his global policies prevailed and served as the basis of a foreign program carried on by succeeding administrations, Republican and Democratic alike. He was the victor on the narrower issue of Korea alone, too, for that war would follow its weary course in the restricted area to which he confined it, and the world would have the precedent—to give it both cold comfort and the material for heated debate—of a limited war kept limited in an atomic era.

But Truman lost a great deal, too, and he lost it on the issue of Korea. He could not bring that war to an end—it would take a new administration to do that. The grudging decision given him in his contest with MacArthur brought him no strength, either in personal prestige or political power. The growing unpopularity of the Korean War became a burden which he would carry the rest of his official life. He would hear it referred to scathingly as "Truman's War." But he displayed no bitterness, because he himself accepted his decisions on Korea as valid measures by which his Administration should be judged. "I wasn't one of the great presidents," he said later, "but I had a hell of a good time trying to be." He said it with the air of a man who believed that history's judgment would be generous.

Truman Was Wrong to Dismiss MacArthur

Courtney Whitney

In the following selection, written in 1955, Courtney Whitney asserts that General Douglas MacArthur's strategy in Korea was superior to President Truman's and that Truman was thus wrong to fire the general. According to Whitney, Truman's emphasis on appeasement and refusal to seek outright victory in the Korean War was a decision that cost thousands of American soldiers their lives. Whitney argues that the years immediately following the Korean War have proven that MacArthur's strategy, which was to battle China in order to prevent the spread of communism in Asia, would have won the Korean War and prevented crises in Indo-China (Vietnam, Laos, and Cambodia). Whitney was a major general who served in both World Wars and the Korean War and was a personal aide to MacArthur.

W HEN THE FIRST COLD NOTICE OF HIS RECALL REACHED Douglas MacArthur in Tokyo, he had not the slightest notion of why the President had taken such action. Now, after a complete investigation by a Senate committee, after countless attempts at an explanation by administration figures involved, and after talks with Americans throughout the length and breadth of the United States, MacArthur still does not know.

Of course it is a larger problem than the relief from

command of one officer, no matter how important his position. The roots of the problem lie much deeper, and the question can be answered only in terms of the great issue of how the Korean war should have been fought.

The Mistake of Passive Defense

Of Truman it may be said that he acted with boldness and decision, however one might rate his judgment, when the North Korean armies struck into the weakly defended south, and by so doing at once commanded the support of the American people and the admiration, as well, of other peoples, particularly in Asia. Had he held to so firm a course when Red China threw down the gauntlet, countless American casualties might have been avoided, the pattern of contemporary events could have been cast in a much more secure and serene mold, and the threat of a new world war would have diminished. But he failed to reject the counsels of fear then thrust upon him; he instead heeded the ill-founded warnings that if we reacted normally and aggressively we would precipitate a world war. And he committed us instead to a course of "passive defense," from which could come only bloodshed with neither victory nor enduring peace.

Those who bore ultimate responsibility for American military and political policy could not, indeed, have served the enemy's cause better than through the formulation and implementation of this extraordinary decision. For it set at the international boundary of Korea a limit upon our military operations which screened from our counterattack or aerial observation the enemy's maneuvers in support of his peninsular campaign. It denied us any right of intrusion upon this sanctuary, even in hot pursuit of enemy aircraft disengaging from combat with our own planes, and prohibited any countermeasures against enemy anti-aircraft batteries emplaced along the north banks of the Yalu to harass our air operations south of the border. It protected the enemy's lines of communication and supply to his peninsular forces by denying us the right by any reasonable means to destroy vital arterial bridges spanning the Yalu or his bases of attack and supply to the north. It facilitated Red Chinese intervention by so doing, and permitted the build-up of a massive Chinese force which, treacherously and without prior notice of belligerency, struck the Eighth Army while advancing to mop up the North Korean remnants. It denied us reinforcement to strengthen our lines even from trained Chinese troops standing by uncommitted on the island of Formosa, while at the same time employing our Seventh Fleet to deny those troops the right to make diversionary attacks upon the common enemy on the Chinese mainland, which would have reduced the pressure upon our beleaguered forces in Korea. It denied us the right to blockade Red China against the importation of supplies essential to sustain its military operations against us. It refused to countenance the employment of our naval and air striking power against Red China's arsenals and other war-sustaining industries, then subject to ready reduction under the weight of our air and naval supremacy, and without which Red China could not have sustained military operations against our forces in Korea, or military adventures elsewhere.

The cumulative effect of these limitations and inhibitions upon the employment of our dominant naval and air potential was to relegate our ground forces in Korea to a costly, unproductive, bloody, and stalemated war of attrition. Because MacArthur could not ask his troops to die for such an indecisive purpose without raising his voice in vigorous protest, he was summarily relieved of his command after, under his leadership and direction, it had regained the initiative against Red China's opposing armies and was even then inflicting crushing and costly local defeats upon them.

Thereafter, at the Soviet's behest, we entered into protracted truce negotiations with the enemy commander, during which, although we discontinued our offensive tactics, we sustained even more casualties than we had suffered during the previous period of active and bitter combat while MacArthur was still in command. Eighty thousand added American casualties—the equivalent of more than five full American infantry divisions—many thousands from within the silence of the grave, sadly attest to this fact. MacArthur estimated that he could have won the war with Red China with less than half this loss had his advice been accepted. These truce talks, with the accompanying easing of our military pressure upon the Red Chinese, permitted them to build up their air power to the point where it could take a much heavier toll of Allied life, to build up their anti-aircraft batteries to the point where they could multiply our own air losses, while at the same time shifting their axis of movement of manpower and supplies to the south as the means of strengthening Communist operations in the reduction of Indo-China and other target areas in southeast Asia. When I told MacArthur of the signing of the Korean Armistice he exclaimed: "This is the death warrant for Indochina."

MacArthur Was Right

All of these developments were clearly foreseen by MacArthur, who repeatedly warned of their inevitability in the wake of any appeasement of our Red Chinese enemy. "In war," he said, "a great nation which does not win must accept all of the consequences of defeat."

Final judgment upon Korean war decisions, although still awaiting events now in the making, has steadily crystallized toward an overwhelming conviction that MacArthur was right and Truman wrong. MacArthur's viewpoint was dictated by his professional judgment, well tested by historic lessons across the panorama of time; Truman's by his rejection of such judgment in the service of what he believed to be the political expediency of the time. MacArthur understood, what Truman did not, that the admixture of military strategy with political expediency can produce national disaster. And he sought to avoid it. He felt, as experience has long taught, that once the diplomats have failed to preserve the peace, it becomes a responsibility of military leadership to devise the strategy which will win the war. Of the soundness of MacArthur's professional acumen it is well to record for the future historian the contemporary estimates expressed after the curtain fell even by those who were hostile to him.

President Truman: "General MacArthur's place in history as one of our greatest commanders is fully established. The nation owes him a debt of gratitude for the distinguished and exceptional service he has rendered our country in posts of great responsibility."

General George Marshall: "He is a man for whom I have tremendous respect as to his military abilities and military performances."

General Omar Bradley (who later admitted that MacArthur might have been right): "I would not say anything to discredit the long and illustrious career of General MacArthur."

General J. Lawton Collins: "I think he is one of the most brilliant military leaders that this country has ever produced. Throughout his career he has been brilliantly successful."

General Hoyt S. Vandenberg: "I have great admiration for him."

Admiral Forrest Sherman: "I would say that he was in the forefront among the strategists with respect to the coordinated use of land, sea and air forces."

General Carl Spaatz, retired Chief of Staff of the Air Force and one of the world's most authoritative strategists, summarized in these words the issue raised when our extraordinary military policy denied MacArthur the right to fight to win:

"Korea," he said, "could have been the right war in the right place. That it did not turn out so can be blamed, in retrospect, on the political limitations placed on the United Nations' objectives, not on the original decision to fight. . . .

"Given the wisdom of hindsight, it now appears that our best opportunity to stop the spread of Communism in Asia was presented to us when the Chinese Communist army crossed the Yalu. This was clearly an act of aggression by Mao Tse-tung fully committing Red China to war and inviting the consequences of that commitment. The United Nations would have been justified in using all the power at its command—land, sea and air—against all the resources under Mao's control, all the way back to the heart of China. History will record the tragic consequences of the U.N. failure to fight Mao with everything we had then and there. When the fighting was stopped in Korea, the Chinese Army had been badly mauled even though its supply lines and resources beyond the Yalu had not been molested. What had started as the first real setback to the Communist march toward domination of Asia, thanks to prompt intervention of U.N. troops spearheaded by the military forces of the U.S., ended in the gratuitous release of Chinese forces and supplies for the fight in Indo-China."

CHAPTER

4

TRUMAN'S
DOMESTIC
POLICIES

The Korean War Diverted Support Away from Truman's Fair Deal

Alonzo L. Hamby

President Franklin D. Roosevelt had developed the New Deal as a response to the Great Depression. Hoping to build upon Roosevelt's domestic achievements, Harry Truman proposed legislation that he named the Fair Deal. Among the goals of the Fair Deal were housing assistance and increases in the minimum wage and unemployment compensation. In the following selection, Alonzo L. Hamby explains why much of the Fair Deal did not come to fruition. According to Hamby, Truman did have some success, including strengthening minimum wage laws and Social Security. However, Congress did not pass the core of the Fair Deal. Hamby asserts that the Korean War was a major reason for the failure of the Fair Deal. He contends that the war—which led to inflation and an obsession with Communist aggression—increased the power of conservative Republicans and prevented Truman from campaigning for liberal Democrats who supported his domestic program. Hamby is a professor of history at Ohio University in Athens, Ohio, and the author of *Man of the People: A Life of Harry S. Truman.*

"**E**VERY SEGMENT OF OUR POPULATION AND EVERY INDIvidual has a right to expect from our Govern-

Excerpted from "The Vital Center, the Fair Deal, and the Quest for a Liberal Political Economy," by Alonzo Hamby, *American Historical Review,* June 1972. Reprinted with permission.

ment a fair deal," declared Harry S. Truman in early 1949. In 1945 and 1946 the Truman administration had almost crumbled under the stresses of postwar reconversion; in 1947 and 1948 it fought a frustrating, if politically rewarding, battle with the Republican Eightieth Congress. Buoyed by his remarkable victory of 1948 and given Democratic majorities in both houses of Congress, Truman hoped to achieve an impressive record of domestic reform. The president systematized his past proposals, added some new ones, and gave his program a name that would both connect his administration with the legacy of the New Deal and give it a distinct identity. The Fair Deal, while based solidly upon the New Deal tradition, differed from its predecessor in significant aspects of mood and detail. It reflected not only Truman's own aspirations but also a style of liberalism that had begun to move beyond the New Deal during World War II and had come to maturity during the early years of the cold war—"the vital center.". . .

The Purpose of the Fair Deal

The Fair Deal was a conscious effort to continue the purpose of the New Deal but not necessarily its methods. Not forced to meet the emergencies of economic depression, given a solid point of departure by their predecessors, and led by a president more prone than FDR to demand programmatic coherence, the Fair Dealers made a systematic effort to discover techniques that would be at once more equitable and more practical in alleviating the problems of unequal wealth and opportunity. Thinking in terms of abundance rather than scarcity, they attempted to adapt the New Deal tradition to postwar prosperity. Seeking to go beyond the New Deal while preserving its objectives, the Truman administration advocated a more sweeping and better-ordered reform agenda. Yet in the quest for political means, Truman and the vital-center liberals could only fall back upon one of the oldest dreams of American

reform—the Jacksonian-Populist vision of a union of producing classes, an invincible farmer-labor coalition. While
superficially plausible, the Fair Deal's political strategy
proved too weak to handle the burden thrust upon it.
The Fair Deal seemed to oscillate between militancy
and moderation. New Dealers had frequently gloried in
accusations of "liberalism" or "radicalism"; Fair Dealers
tended to shrink from such labels. The New Dealers had
often lusted for political combat; the Fair Dealers were
generally more low keyed. Election campaigns demanded
an aggressiveness that would arouse the Democratic presidential party, but the continued strength of the conservative coalition in Congress dictated accommodation in the
post-election efforts to secure passage of legislative proposals. Such tactics reflected Truman's personal political
experience and instincts, but they also developed naturally
out of the climate of postwar America. The crisis of economic depression had produced one style of political
rhetoric; the problems of prosperity and inflation brought
forth another.

The Fair Deal mirrored Truman's policy preferences
and approach to politics; it was no more the president's
personal creation, however, than the New Deal had been
Roosevelt's. Just as FDR's advisers had formulated much of
the New Deal, a group of liberals developed much of the
content and tactics of the Fair Deal. For the most part
these were the men who had formed a liberal caucus within the administration in early 1947 shortly after the Republican triumph in the congressional elections of 1946,
had worked to sway the president toward the left in his
policy recommendations and campaign tactics, and had
played a significant, if not an all-embracing, role in Truman's victory in 1948. Truman's special counsel, Clark M.
Clifford, was perhaps the most prominent member of the
group, but Clifford, although a shrewd political analyst, a
persuasive advocate, and an extremely valuable adminis-

trative chief of staff, was neither the caucus's organizer nor a creative liberal thinker. Others gave the Fair Deal its substance as a program descending from the New Deal yet distinct from it. . . .

Obstacles to the Fair Deal

During 1949 and early 1950 the Truman administration managed a record of substantial legislative accomplishment, but it consisted almost entirely of additions to such New Deal programs as the minimum wage, social security, and public power. The Housing Act of 1949, with its provisions for large-scale public housing, appeared to be a breakthrough, but weak administration, local opposition, and inadequate financing subsequently vitiated hopes that it would help the poor. Acting on his executive authority, Truman took an important step by forcing the army to agree to a policy of desegregation. The heart of the Fair Deal, however—repeal of the Taft-Hartley Act [a law passed in 1947 that significantly limited the rights and powers of unions], civil rights legislation, aid to education, national medical insurance, and the Brannan Plan [a policy developed by Secretary of Agriculture Charles Brannan to prevent the concentration of production in the hands of a few farmers]—failed in Congress. Given the power of the well-entrenched conservative coalition and a widespread mood of public apathy about big new reforms, Truman could only enlarge upon the record of his predecessor.

Democratic strategists hoped for a mandate in the congressional elections of 1950. In the spring Truman made a successful whistle-stop tour of the West and Midwest, rousing party enthusiasm and apparently demonstrating a solid personal popularity. A.J. Loveland's victory provided further encouragement, and in California the aggressive Fair Dealer Helen Gahagan Douglas won the Democratic nomination for the Senate by a thumping margin. Two incumbent Fair Deal supporters—Frank Graham of North Carolina and Claude Pepper of Florida—lost their senatorial primaries, but, as Southerners who had run afoul of the race issue, they did not seem to be indicators of national trends. Nevertheless, the hope of cutting into the strength of the conservative opposition ran counter to the historical pattern of mid-term elections. The beginning of the Korean War at the end of June destroyed any chances of success.

How the War Hurt the Administration

The most immediate impact of Korea was to refuel an anti-Communist extremism that might otherwise have sputtered out. Senator Joseph McCarthy had begun his rise to prominence in February 1950, but he had failed to prove any of his multiple allegations and seemed definitively discredited by the investigations of a special Senate committee headed by Millard Tydings. McCarthy, it is true, was a talented demagogue who should have been taken more seriously by the liberals and the Truman administration in early 1950, but it seems probable that his appeal would have waned more quickly if the cold war with communism had not suddenly become hot. As it was, many of his Senate colleagues rushed to emulate him. In September 1950 Congress passed the McCarran Internal Security Act; only a handful of congressional liberals dared dissent from the overwhelming vote in favor. Truman's subsequent veto was intelligent and courageous, but was issued more for the history books than with any real hope of success. In the subsequent campaign, liberal Democrats, whether they had voted for the McCarran Act [passed in 1950, it required the registration of all Communist organizations, among other provisions] or not, found themselves facing charges of softness toward communism.

The war hurt the administration in other ways. It touched off a brief but serious inflation, which caused widespread consumer irritation. By stimulating demand for agricultural products it brought most farm prices up to parity levels and thereby undercut whatever attractiveness the Brannan Plan had developed in rural areas. Finally it removed the Democratic party's most effective spokesman—the president—from active participation in the campaign. Forced to play the role of war leader, Truman allowed himself only one major partisan speech, delivered in St. Louis on the eve of the balloting.

The November 1950 Congressional Elections

The Fair Deal might have been a winning issue in a nation oriented toward domestic concerns and recovering from an economic recession; it had much less appeal in a country obsessed with Communist aggression and experiencing an inflationary war boom. The reaction against the administration was especially strong in the Midwest. Indiana's Democratic aspirant for the Senate asked Oscar Ewing to stay out of the state. In Iowa, Loveland desperately attempted to reverse his identification with the Brannan Plan. In Missouri the managers of senatorial candidate Thomas C. Hennings, Jr. privately asked White House aides to make Truman's St. Louis speech a foreign policy address that would skip lightly over Fair Deal issues. A few days before the election the columnist Stewart Alsop returned from a Midwestern trip convinced that the region had never been more conservative. Nevertheless, Truman's political advisers, and probably Truman himself, felt that the Fair Deal still had appeal. Given the basic strength of the economy and the victories in Korea that followed the Inchon landing, the White House believed that the Democrats could easily rebut generalized charges of fumbling or softness toward communism. In mid-October the Democratic National Committee and many local leaders were so confident of success that their main concern was simply to get out the vote.

The November results, however, showed a Democratic loss of twenty-eight seats in the House of Representatives and five seats in the Senate. Truman seized every opportunity to remind all who would listen that the numbers were small by traditional mid-term standards. Liberal political

Truman's Economic Accomplishments

In the following excerpt from his biography Truman, *David McCullough details the ways in which the American economy improved during the Truman presidency.*

A new census report [in 1952] confirmed that gains in income, standards of living, education, and housing since Truman took office were unparalleled in American history. As Truman would report in his final State of the Union message to Congress, on January 7, 1953, 62 million Americans had jobs, which was a gain of 11 million jobs in seven years. Unemployment had all but disappeared. Farm income, corporate income, and dividends were at an all-time high. There had not been a failure of an insured bank in nearly nine years. His most important accomplishments, he knew, were in world affairs. Yet he could rightly point with pride to the fact that the postwar economic collapse that everyone expected never happened, that through government support (the GI Bill) 8 million veterans had been to college, that Social Security benefits had been doubled, the minimum wage increased. There had been progress in slum clearance, millions of homes built through government financing. Prices were higher, but incomes, for the most part, had risen even more. Real living standards were considerably higher than seven years earlier.

Truman had failed to do as much as he wanted for public housing, education, failed to establish the medical insurance program he knew the nation needed, but he had battled hard for these programs, set goals for the future.

David McCullough, *Truman*. New York: Simon & Schuster, 1992.

analysts, including Kenneth Hechler, a White House staffer, and Gus Tyler of the International Ladies Garment Workers Union, subjected the returns to close scrutiny and all but pronounced a Democratic victory. All the same, most of the Democrats who went under had been staunch Fair Dealers. Republican candidates, including John Marshall Butler in Maryland, Richard M. Nixon in California, Everett McKinley Dirksen in Illinois, and Robert A. Taft in Ohio, scored some of the most spectacular GOP victories by blending right-wing conservatism with McCarthyism. The Midwestern losses were especially disappointing. Hechler argued that the corn-belt vote primarily reflected urban defections and that the Democrats had done comparatively well among farmers. Perhaps so, but for all practical purposes the results put an end to the Brannan strategy of constructing a farmer-labor coalition. Truman was probably more accurate than Hechler when, with characteristic overstatement, he privately expressed his disappointment: "The main trouble with the farmers is that they hate labor so badly that they will not vote for their own interests."

Truman Quietly Shelves His Legislative Program

Thereafter, with the Chinese intervention transforming the Korean War into a more serious conflict and with the dismissal of General Douglas MacArthur in April 1951, Truman faced a tough attack from a Republican opposition determined to capitalize upon the frustrations of Korea. Finding it necessary to place party unity above all else, he quietly shelved most of his domestic legislative program and sought to bring the conservative wing of his party behind his military and defense policies. He secretly asked Richard B. Russell of Georgia, the kingpin of the Southern conservatives, to assume the Democratic leadership in the Senate. Russell, content with the substance of power, declined and gave his nod to Ernest W. McFarland of Arizona, an amiable tool of the Southern bloc; Truman made no effort to prevent McFarland's selection as Senate majority leader. The president's State of the Union message was devoted almost entirely to foreign policy and defense mobilization and mentioned social welfare programs only as an afterthought. Subsequently Truman told a press conference that while he supported the Fair Deal as much as ever, "first things come first, and our defense programs must have top priority.". . .

In its effort to carry on with the reforming impulse of the New Deal the Truman administration faced nearly insuperable obstacles. A loosely knit but nonetheless effective conservative coalition had controlled Congress since 1939, successfully defying Franklin Roosevelt long before it had to deal with Truman. Postwar prosperity muted economic liberalism and encouraged a mood of apathy toward new reform breakthroughs, although Truman's victory in 1948 indicated that most of the elements of the old Roosevelt coalition were determined to preserve the gains of the New Deal. The cold war probably made it more difficult to focus public attention upon reform and dealt severe blows to civil liberties. It did, however, give impetus to the movement for Negro equality.

Truman Failed to Support Liberal Causes

Charles Peters

Charles Peters, the founder and editor-in-chief of the *Washington Monthly*, contends that President Truman was not a crusader for liberal causes, as many of his admirers contend. In the following essay, Peters writes that despite having a Democratic majority in the House and Senate after the 1948 elections, Truman did not try to get liberal programs enacted. Peters suggests that Truman's proposed Fair Deal was a cynical ploy to win the election and did not reflect the president's true convictions. Peters also criticizes Truman's decision to institute a loyalty program and his attitudes toward civil rights. Peters asserts that Truman's cronyism and lack of sophistication are further reasons why the president failed to inspire America and its citizens to greater achievements.

D AVID MCCULLOUGH'S HIGHLY READABLE BIOGRAPHY PAYS proper respect to Harry Truman's greatest achievements, beginning with the Truman Committee, where, as a senator, he proved it possible for Congress to effectively monitor government programs, and continuing through the high points of his presidency: the Marshall Plan, Point Four, the Berlin airlift, desegregation of the armed forces, recognition of Israel, resistance to aggression in South Korea, and the firing of MacArthur. Of these, the two that

Excerpted from "Mild About Harry: How Truman Ushered in the End of Liberal Idealism," by Charles Peters, *The Washington Monthly*, June 1992. Reprinted with permission from *The Washington Monthly*. Copyright by The Washington Monthly Company, 1611 Connecticut Ave. NW, Washington, DC 20009; (202) 462-0128; www.washingtonmonthly.com.

have been most underappreciated are the Truman Committee and the Berlin airlift.

The Truman Committee demonstrated through its constructive criticism of wartime defense spending that Congress can oversee other branches of government. Today, sadly, that kind of oversight is almost a lost art. Truman's wise decision to supply Soviet-blockaded Berlin through the air, instead of confronting strong Soviet ground forces, ranks along with Kennedy's handling of the Cuban Missile Crisis as a landmark example of how to be resolute without going to war.

McCullough also acknowledges Truman's negatives, but he does so—and this is his book's main defect—with little explanation of their significance, either at the time or in the broader context of history.

The Mistakes of the Truman Administration

While Truman was a lovable man who will forever stand out among our presidents for his humanity and courage, he made many mistakes, some of them whoppers. By excluding South Korea from a defense perimeter he announced in 1949, his secretary of state, Dean Acheson, may have signaled the North Koreans that they could invade South Korea. Truman's administration also misjudged China's threats that it would enter the Korean War if the United States crossed the 38th parallel and approached the Yalu River.

On the domestic scene, Truman, although not by any means a Joe McCarthy, instituted unduly restrictive classification and loyalty programs in the federal government. He also nominated two justices to the Supreme Court, Fred Vinson and Tom Clark, who became part of the majority that upheld in the Dennis case the imprisonment of American Communist Party leaders simply for teaching and advocating Marxist doctrine—a decision that, for me, marks the low point in the history of the First Amendment. These actions were crucial in creating the climate of conformity that dominated the fifties, and they did permanent damage to the civil and foreign services by greatly heightening the customary caution of the bureaucrat.

Truman's administration was also characterized by cronyism (Harry Vaughan and Donald Dawson [White House aide and Truman administrative assistant, respectively] were unhappy examples), by terrible judgment in the appointment of such cabinet members as Louis Johnson as secretary of defense and J. Howard McGrath as attorney general, and by a too-easy tolerance of corruption that probably was the result of Truman's adjustment to his role in the Pendergast machine in Kansas City early in his political life. [Thomas J. Pendergast was a Missouri politician whose political machine had considerable power over Kansas City's Democrats.] (He managed to survive as personally incorruptible by winking at the shenanigans of others.) He was also guilty of a shoot-from-the-lip carelessness, as when he declared during the Korean War that he thought the use of the atomic bomb could be left to the discretion of the military commanders in the field.

Truman Did Not Push Liberal Causes

But my most severe indictment of Truman is that he inflicted the first wound in the slow death of liberal idealism in America that began in 1945. For the first 45 years of this century, idealism was a vibrant force, and for 28 of those 45 years, we had inspiring leaders—Theodore Roosevelt, Woodrow Wilson, and FDR. In the 45 years since, we've had only the period between 1961 and 1965, when the New Frontier and the Great Society briefly revived a spirit of generosity and hope before that spirit was crushed by Vietnam and Watergate.

The truth is that Truman was generally not a crusader for liberal causes. With respect to civil rights, for example, he sought a plank for his platform that was "mild and ambiguous enough to mollify" segregationists. In private, he called blacks "niggers" and referred to civil rights advocate Hubert Humphrey as "a crackpot." Liberals, as a result, deserted him and tried in the spring of 1948 to persuade Dwight Eisenhower to run as a Democrat that year. When that effort failed, many then supported the third-party candidacy of Henry Wallace.

It was only during the final month of the 1948 campaign that Truman's message was passionately liberal and he really captured the hearts of the non-communist left. Ordinarily critical columnists, like the *New Republic*'s TRB and the *New Yorker*'s Richard Rovere, said kind things about him. And I can still remember how excited I, who had been prepared to vote for Wallace earlier in the campaign, became during October and how intensely I was rooting for Truman to win on election night when the pundits were predicting a Dewey victory.

The most telling test of Truman's liberalism was what he did with his triumph. As 1949 began, he was no longer handcuffed by a Republican Congress. He had Democratic majorities in both houses. So did he seize the moment and move with bold resolution to get liberal programs enacted?

A Failure to Try

The answer provided by McCullough, who is unaware of the negative implication of what he is saying: "The first six months of the new term were a breather for Truman."

Instead of twisting arms on Capitol Hill, in March he flew off to Key West for another "working vacation," which was truly Reaganesque since he had already rested in the Keys just after the fall election—and doesn't seem to have returned to the White House until May. Here's McCullough's again uncritical description of how the days were spent:

> He basked in the sun with members of his staff, listened to music on the phonograph, took an afternoon nap,

played poker on the porch every night, and started off each day with a shot of bourbon before his walk. The staff all enjoyed themselves, as did the 30-odd reporters who usually made the trips and had little to do but enjoy themselves.

It could be argued that, because there were quite a few Dixiecrats in Truman's congressional majority, he would have had difficulty getting a legislative program passed. But he should have tried. Not trying proved that his campaign rhetoric had been cynical, a liberalism adopted not out of conviction but out of the desire to be reelected. Indeed, liberalism had been proposed as a 1948 campaign strategy by the famous Clifford memorandum (now revealed to have originally been drafted by Jim Rowe). It recommended special appeals to groups such as farmers, labor unions, blacks, Catholics, Italians, and Jews. It may have been the intellectual godfather of the interest-group liberalism that was to be the curse of the Democratic Party for the next several decades.

A Failure to Inspire

Truman's cynicism was not the only factor in his failure to inspire. He often seemed embarrassing. This was part his fault, part the people's.

Truman considered himself "a plain man," which was the way most Americans thought of themselves in 1945. But developments were underway that would cause many of them to identify with the upper classes and to begin to see their president as the father whose social lapses are excruciating to his adolescent children, who aspire to higher society.

One of the truly transforming changes in American history began the year Truman became president. In the fall of 1945, veterans swarmed to the nation's universities to take advantage of the GI Bill. Millions who would otherwise have been unable to afford to do so acquired college degrees. This radically elevated the educational level of the American people and it provided a passport into the middle of the middle class for many who otherwise would have been doomed to the lower rungs. Yet mass access to college also subtly devalued the bachelor's degree, and cultural taste began to replace that degree as a way of proving class. In the late forties, the popularity of the *New Yorker,* which taught lessons in taste, soared, as did the appeal of similarly enriching trips through Europe.

My favorite example of this change is the contrast between the popularity of two Broadway productions. In the 1945–46 theater season, a splendid revival of *Pygmalion* survived only a few months, despite great performances by Gertrude Lawrence as Eliza and Melville Cooper as Doolittle, while a decade later *My Fair Lady* reigned as the smash hit of the era. The music of Lerner and Loewe was certainly part of the explanation. But another factor that contributed to the popularity of *My Fair Lady* was that its underlying message—that style could be acquired—was enthusiastically embraced by a public that was now eager to hear it.

A Failure to Touch the Soul

Harry Truman indisputably lacked style. In fact, he seemed to scorn it. Perhaps the most infamous illustration of this indifference was his letter to the *Washington Post*'s music critic, Paul Hume, after Hume wrote an unflattering review of a recital at Constitution Hall by Truman's daughter, Margaret, who was then attempting a career on the concert stage:

> Mr. Hume: I've just read your lousy review of Margaret's concert. I've come to the conclusion that you are an 'eight ulcer man on four ulcer pay.'
>
> It seems to me you are a frustrated old man [Hume was 34] who wishes he could have been successful. When

you write such poppycock as was in the back section of the paper you work for, it shows conclusively that you're off the beam and at least four of your ulcers are at work.

Some day I hope to meet you. When that happens you'll need a new nose, a lot of beef-steak for black eyes, and perhaps a supporter below!

Westbrook Pegler, a gutter snipe, is a gentleman beside you. I hope you'll accept that statement as a worse insult than a reflection on your ancestry.

The spirit poured into this letter represents precisely what made Truman lovable, and considered in that light, some of the language is forgivable. But, taken as a whole, the letter is so sadly distant from the language of a Churchill or a DeGaulle or a Roosevelt that one can understand how it troubled even those indifferent to social status.

If there is a lesson to be learned from the leadership of Harry Truman, it is that there is nothing wrong with having a plain man as president. Indeed, after watching the taste-makes-class game reach its ultimate absurdity in the vanities of the eighties, even the snobs have to admit that there is much that is attractive about the prospect of a plain-man president. But we also need for him to be someone who refuses to appeal to our selfishness, who instead summons the best that is within us with words that touch our souls. However admirable Harry Truman was in many ways, this is a test that he failed. It is a test Abraham Lincoln passed.

Truman Helped Advance Civil Rights

Donald R. McCoy and Richard T. Ruetten

Truman was the first president to have a civil rights program. In the following essay, Donald R. McCoy and Richard T. Ruetten argue that while Truman's civil rights record was not perfect, he did advance the cause of minorities. In 1946, he appointed the President's Committee on Civil Rights, which studied the problems facing minorities. Due largely to that committee, the federal government became more aware of discrimination and took steps to reduce biases in the schools and workplace. Racial minorities also benefited from the expansion of social-welfare programs and Truman's expansion of Franklin Roosevelt's desegregation of the military. However, the authors write that opposition to civil rights was too strong in the 1940s and 1950s to prevent more from being achieved. When they wrote this essay in 1973, McCoy was a professor of history at the University of Kansas and Ruetten was a history professor at San Diego State University.

A LTHOUGH THE ADAPTATION OF MINORITIES TO AMERICAN life has been varied, by the 1930s most immigrant groups had attained or approached equality of opportunity and rights. It was a different story, however, for those who because of color, geographical origins, or religion differed considerably in their backgrounds from the vast majority of Americans.

The 1930s marked a change in the trends affecting most of the nation's minorities, largely because of the New Deal's efforts to ameliorate their plight. Discrimination and segregation, however, were still standard principles in 1940 in the United States. Only Jews, chiefly because of their European background and advanced skills, were close to the economic and political means of American life. The condition of most Negroes, Indians, Mexican-Americans, and Oriental-Americans was still pitiful.

The Second World War brought substantial changes in the position of the minorities. All except Japanese-Americans profited from the prosperity generated by war production, and military service benefited many of the nonwhites who wore the nation's uniform. By 1945, minority-group employment and income stood at record levels, more opportunities for advancement had appeared, further skills had been acquired, and the National Association for the Advancement of Colored People was emerging as a major political force. Equally important, minority-group leaders resolved not only that their people should keep what they had gained but that they should press harder for equality. In this they sought, with some success, to ally with one another and with sympathetic elements among the majority of Americans.

1946 as a Turning Point

There were some signs that civil-rights gains would continue in the postwar period. After Franklin Roosevelt's death in 1945, the new president, Harry S. Truman, urged Congress to establish a permanent Fair Employment Practices Commission (FEPC) and appointed Irvin C. Mollison to the Customs Court, the highest judicial position at that time for an American Negro. Yet, hope soon receded for minorities. They not only experienced cutbacks in jobs but had to compete in the shrinking job market with returning soldiers and sailors. With increasing unemployment and rapid demobilization came mounting racial tensions. Particularly in the South and West, many returning minority-group servicemen faced indignities, intimidation, and even violence. Urban housing, already cramped because of large-scale migration to the cities, worsened as demobilization progressed. Despite strenuous efforts by civil-rights lobbyists, all civil-rights measures before Congress failed, except for the Indian Claims Commission Act of 1946.

It was violence, however, the unwarranted assaults on blacks in 1946, that regenerated civil-rights progress. Outraged, Negro leaders demanded action; and they were supported by a surge of concern among whites. The Department of Justice and the White House sought to curb attacks on nonwhites. Because of the inadequacy of federal laws, however, the government had only a paper sword to wield in the form of investigations and prosecutions, but that at least harassed alleged assailants. Pressure was also brought to bear on southern governors to uphold state laws. Whether these actions, and the nation's shocked reaction to the assaults, were primarily responsible for the calming of tensions remains arguable. Nevertheless, racial violence declined during the latter part of 1946 and remained on a low level for five years.

In effect, 1946 was a turning point, if only because of a conjunction of pressure from indignant civil-rights groups with rising White House determination to forestall a reoccurrence of the racial violence and intolerance that had marred the post–World War I period. And this was set against the willingness of public opinion for some action on civil rights. The immediate result was the scrutinizing of the whole range of minority problems, mainly through the instrumentality of the President's Committee on Civil Rights, which Truman appointed late in 1946.

Truman's Reform Efforts

There is no need here to itemize the actions of the Truman administration or the civil-rights advances in the various sectors of American life. The results can be discussed by categories. The president became the prime educator for the need to secure the rights and dignity of all citizens, and he strove to make opportunity and treatment more nearly equal for minorities in the civil service and the armed forces. He worked, though with little success, for enactment of a cohesive civil-rights program and, with greater success, to block legislation that would jeopardize minority interests. Truman also made occasional appointments of minority-group members to public offices and sought to heighten self-government in America's territories. The federal government became increasingly sensitive to complaints about discrimination in discharging public services. The Justice Department encouraged law officers everywhere to give an even break to minority peoples and intervened, through its amicus curiae briefs, to gain favorable court decisions in civil-rights cases. Like Truman, the department came to accept the argument that segregation and discrimination were inseparable problems, for segregation was a pattern that fostered and perpetuated discrimination. The Supreme Court, building on earlier decisions that had combated the widespread disenfranchisement of nonwhites and segregation in Pullman cars and interstate buses, responded in a series of cases that withdrew the legal bases for restrictive covenants, unequal school facilities, and segregated railway dining cars. Progress also occurred on state and local levels, as an increasing number of laws and ordinances struck at discrimination in hiring, public housing, schooling, and the use of public facilities. Some change came in private areas, as minorities increasingly participated in a wider variety of activities and jobs. Noteworthy was the extent to which civil rights and minorities became acceptable themes in literature and public discussions; and highly significant were Hollywood's changing image of the Negro and the breakthrough of blacks in organized athletics.

These developments, together with advances in social-security benefits, minimum-wage levels, and health programs, constituted a substantial step forward. Minorities, particularly Negroes, occupied a place in government planning and programs as they never had before. They saw heartening responses to their pressures and, from time to time, even tangible results. The pace of change and encouragement had quickened beyond what their leaders had envisaged in 1945.

Why Progress Was Achieved

Progress came about for a number of reasons. Thanks considerably to wartime gains, minority groups—especially Jews and Negroes—now had the money, inspiration, organization, and leaders to fight for advancement. And they had the goals. America's wartime propaganda had held these goals on high; and this reinforced and refined what minority citizens had been telling themselves for years. Moreover, the spate of books and articles on minority problems, beginning in 1940, had well publicized their plight and potential. Migration, especially of blacks to the North, and the growing number of minority-group citizens who could vote honed their sensitivity to the possibility of change and heightened their political power. Minorities were all the stronger because of their informal postwar coalition and because of the greater concern of white liberals and a number of religious and labor leaders, who acted sometimes out of principle and sometimes in search of quid pro quo. In short, minorities had gained a secure foothold in the foothills of American democracy, enabling them to exert pressure that could be felt in the cold high range of the nation's institutions.

Crucial to effective minority pressure was the fact that government was more than ever receptive to it. Harry S. Truman was a man intent upon further securing constitutional guarantees to all Americans—a man who wanted to do, as he often said, "the right thing." Here, too, was a president who increasingly turned to advisers who were not only sympathetic to the quest for equal rights and opportunities, but were also keenly aware of the political advantages, at home and abroad, of assisting that quest. At home, the administration would gain more leverage with congressional liberals, the bedrock of support for the Fair Deal legislative program. The administration's stand on civil rights also strengthened it in vying for liberal and minority-group backing in Truman's bid for nomination and election in 1948. Abroad, America was under serious attack from international communism and from the emerging nonwhite nations because of the gap between its principles and practices in racial matters. As the cold war developed, the Truman administration sought to blunt communism's exploitation of the issue in order to enlist allies from among the new nations, or at least to keep them uncommitted.

The application of nonwhite pressure and the frequently positive response to it during the Truman years were aided by the increasing disposition of some white, Christian Americans to favor progress for minority groups. They were sickened by the brutality of Nazism and had accepted the egalitarian teachings of political liberals and leftists. Many Americans, especially among the young, read of the plight of minorities; some of them came increasingly in contact with Negroes, Jews, Mexican-Americans, Indians, and Oriental-Americans and found that they were in no way diminished or threatened.

The upshot was not a revolution in the lives of America's minority peoples, but by the end of the Truman administration substantial progress had been made. Although Congress had not enacted a fair employment practices law, by 1953 twelve states and thirty cities had adopted such legislation, though it was of varying effectiveness. The general conclusion of studies of fair employment legislation was that where it was enforced, it had an impact in reducing racial and religious discrimination in employment. Of course, the labor requirements of the Korean War, President Truman's wartime National Manpower Mobilization Policy, and especially his Committee on Government Contract Compliance supplemented the work of fair employment agencies and private groups, such as the Urban League.

Advances in Work and Education

Generally favorable employment needs and public and private pressures for fair hiring practices created an unusually favorable job situation for minorities. Employment and income rates after World War II remained considerably higher than prewar levels. The coming of the Korean War opened opportunities even wider, and minorities experienced relatively little trouble in finding jobs of some kind. As of 1953, only 4.1 percent of the nonwhite labor force was unemployed, compared to 2.3 percent of whites. Median nonwhite family income rose from $1,614 to $2,338 between 1947 and 1952; and that income grew in its percentage of median white family income from 51 to 57—a record. There was also a great shift in the occupational categories of black Americans, from 19.3 percent in 1940 in professional, white collar, skilled, and semiskilled work to 37.1 by 1950.

Other advances were evident by the end of the Truman administration. Racial minorities benefited from social-welfare measures, such as the 1950 amendments to the Social Security Act, which liberalized payments and covered additional workers, and health and minimum-wage programs. Some progress was made in opening eating places, hotels, parks, and theaters to minorities, although it was uneven and small in terms of the number of people affected. Some unions eliminated or relaxed their discriminatory practices. With little fanfare, the American Medical Association and many medical specialist societies dropped racial bars to membership; and by 1953 twenty-seven medical associations in six southern states and the District of Columbia had black members, whereas none had had any in 1947. Only one state nursing association refused Negro members by 1954. The nonwhite life-expectancy age jumped from 53.1 in 1940 to 61.7 in 1953, compared to 64.2 and 69.6 for whites over the same period. The gap was still monstrous, but it was closing.

BELL-RINGER

Herb Lock © 1948 The Washington Post Co.

There were dramatic changes in schooling, too. The percentage of nonwhites from ages five to nineteen who were enrolled in school rose from 68.4 to 74.8, and of whites from 75.6 to 79.3, between 1940 and 1950. The median of school years completed increased during the decade from 5.7 to 7 for nonwhites and from 8.7 to 9.7 for whites; and the percentage of nonwhites in high school and college rose from 16.7 in 1940 to 20.6 in 1950. Indeed, [Carter Godwin] Woodson and [Charles Harris] Wesley report that the number of Negroes in institutions of higher education had increased between 1940 and 1950 from 23,000 to 113,735. Partly because of fear that the Supreme Court would force integration in schools, southern states greatly expanded the outlay for Negro education between 1940 and 1952, with the per-pupil expenditure in nine states rising from $21.54 to $115.08, and capital outlay per pupil increasing from $.99 to $29.58, although the dollar increases for white schools were a bit larger. The gap in twelve southern states in the number of years of college training received by white and black teachers narrowed, however, and the dollar increase in average salaries for teachers was slightly larger for Negroes, rising $1,902 compared to $1,846 for whites.

Furthermore, owner-occupied dwellings of nonwhites increased from 23.6 to 34.9 percent between 1940 and 1950, compared to 45.7 and 57 percent for whites. A veritable revolution occurred in the military services, accelerated by President Truman's actions and the Korean War, which was revealed primarily in greater desegregation, integration, and opportunity, but also in racial proportions of manpower strength. In the army the percentage of black officers grew from 1.7 to 2.9, and of enlisted men from 9.6 to 12.3, between 1949 and 1953; air force figures showed an increase in black officers from 0.6 to 1.1 percent, and of Negro enlisted men from 5.1 to 8.6 percent. The marines and the navy went from virtually no black officers to precious few; and although the percentage of black enlisted men in the navy declined, it rose substantially in the Marine Corps—from 2.1 to 6.5. In short, desegregation of the military was one of the most significant breakthroughs in civil rights in the twentieth century.

The First President to Have a Civil-Rights Program

That more was not accomplished during the Truman years was disappointing and regrettable in terms of social justice and national welfare. Plainly, not enough whites were willing to go much further in combating discrimination and its effects through private actions or the work of state and local governments, and minorities did not possess sufficient strength to force more progress. The spur of civil-rights advocates was compelling, but the bridle of their opponents was almost proportionately discouraging. As black men struggled to rise economically, politically, and socially in the postwar period, they found themselves increasingly in competition with whites, many of whom felt such confrontation threatening and impossible to accept. Little more could have been expected of Congress, which did little, and of the Supreme Court, which accomplished much. The White House might have dared more—for example, a thoroughgoing attack on discrimination in the civil service and in the rendering of public services, additional appointments of minority-group officeholders and actively sympathetic whites, and the earlier formation of the Committee on Government Contract Compliance (with better financial support). Yet although Harry Truman often moved by fits and starts and left something to be desired, he was the first president to have a civil-rights program, the first to try to come to grips with the basic problems of minorities, and the first to condemn, vigorously and consistently, the presence of discrimination and inequality in America. His endeavors, courage, and accomplishments far surpassed those of his predecessors, and at a time when it would not have been difficult to have treated the civil-rights problem with soft soap alone. The record of the Truman years showed the strength of the American system in that progress was made; but it also revealed society's weakness in its inability, in a whirlpool of conflicting interests and pressures, to move forward either rapidly or wisely enough.

1953 and Its Aftermath

Nevertheless, the position of minorities in 1953 had improved. Jews rarely gave signs of feeling like an aggrieved or besieged minority. Oriental-Americans had moved forward on all fronts, so that today, for example, Japanese-Americans are more middle class than the white majority in terms of education and accomplishment. To be sure, most Indians and Mexican-Americans could complain that matters had not changed markedly for them; and the Puerto Ricans, who had flocked to the mainland to gain their fortunes, had received little. The largest minority by far—black Americans—had gained considerably, however inadequate their advances appear today.

In 1923 had minority leaders been told that the following year their people would possess what they did in 1953, it would have seemed a fantastic achievement. But what black, brown, and red Americans actually enjoyed in 1953 fell far short of fulfilling their aspirations. They too were children of the American heritage. Franklin Roosevelt made the same golden promises to them that he did to whites, and Harry Truman singled out the racial minorities for attention in 1948. The minority peoples knew, as they had witnessed during depression and war, what government could do when it applied its power. They saw the life styles of whites as depicted in motion pictures, advertising, and television. The lessening of discrimination, segregation, and violence was fine as far as it went; so was the increase in opportunities, income, and freedom. But these were not enough, and they were not all that the nation could give. It was clear that America had an obligation to grant more in order to provide the equality under law that it had for generations been promising. Moreover, in view of the cold war, the emergence of nonwhite nations, and the need for domestic stability, the United States could not afford less than full payment of its promises to all citizens—throughout the country, and soon.

Yet, by 1953, the omens were mixed. A new president had made promises, but Congress gave no signs of being less intransigent than in preceding years. Moreover, the civil-rights coalition had been seriously weakened as anti-Semitism diminished and Jews became increasingly caught up in the affairs of Israel and as Japanese-Americans became better integrated into society. During the 1950s, much of the energy of Democratic liberals was spent in combating McCarthyism and, after 1952, in efforts to regain political power. Many civil-rights advocates flagged in their work, stung by repeated charges of communism and even harassment by government agencies. Minorities also were hindered by the repeated declarations that in a prosperous nation, they too *must* be prospering. Blacks found themselves increasingly alone in the civil-rights struggle; and Indians, Mexican-Americans, and Puerto Ricans were seldom in a position to help themselves, much less to help revivify the civil-rights coalition. During the Eisenhower years, some progress was made in education and home ownership. There were also the desegregation decision in *Brown v. Board of Education of Topeka*, rudimentary civil-rights legislation in 1957 and 1960, and advances in completing integration in the armed forces. The pace of progress, however, had plainly fallen off.

Truman Was Overly Cautious in His Civil Rights Agenda

Barton J. Bernstein

In the following selection, Barton J. Bernstein maintains that President Truman was overly cautious in his efforts to strengthen civil rights. Bernstein acknowledges that Truman took several important steps, including appointing a committee to study the issue of discrimination. However, Bernstein argues that Truman failed to use his executive powers to make the improvements suggested by the committee. Bernstein also contends that Truman moderated his views on civil rights in order to retain Southern Democrats during the 1948 election. Bernstein is a professor of American history at Stanford University in Palo Alto, California, and the editor of various books, including *Towards a New Past: Dissenting Essays in American History*, from which this viewpoint has been excerpted.

I N COURTING THE NEGRO THE TRUMAN ADMINISTRATION IN 1948 made greater promises to black citizens than had any previous federal government in American history. Yet, like many Americans, Truman as a senator had regarded the Negro's plight as peripheral to his interests, and with many of his generation he believed that equality was compatible with segregation. As President, however, he found

Excerpted from "America in War and Peace: The Test of Liberalism," by Barton J. Bernstein in *Towards a New Past: Dissenting Essays in American History*, edited by Barton J. Bernstein. Copyright © 1968 by Random House, Inc. Used by permission of Pantheon Books, a division of Random House, Inc.

himself slowly prodded by conscience and pushed by politics. He moved cautiously at first and endorsed only measures affirming legal equality and protecting Negroes from violence.

Reluctant to Take a Stand

Reluctant to fragment the crumbling Democratic coalition, Truman, in his first year, had seemed to avoid taking positions on civil rights which might upset the delicate balance between Northern and Southern Democrats. While he endorsed legislation for a statutory Federal Employment Practices Committee (FEPC) that the Congress would not grant, his efforts on behalf of the temporary FEPC (created by Roosevelt's executive order) were weaker. Having already weakened the power of the temporary agency, he also acquiesced in the legislative decision to kill it. Despite the fears of Negro leaders that the death of FEPC would leave Negroes virtually unprotected from discrimination in the postwar job market, Truman would not even issue an order requiring nondiscrimination in the federal service and by government contractors.

Though Truman was unwilling to use the prestige or power of his great office significantly on behalf of Negroes, he did assist their cause. While sidestepping political conflict, he occasionally supported FEPC and abolition of the poll tax. When Negroes were attacked, he did condemn the racial violence. Though generally reluctant to move beyond rhetoric during his early years, Truman, shortly before the 1946 election, found conscience and politics demanding more. So distressed was he by racial violence that when Walter White of the NAACP and a group of white liberals urged him to assist the Negro, he promised to create a committee to study civil rights.

The promise of a committee could have been a device to resist pressures, to delay the matter until after the election. And Truman could have appointed a group of politically safe men of limited reputation—men he could control. But instead, after the election, perhaps in an effort to mobilize the liberals for 1948, he appointed a committee of prominent men sympathetic to civil rights. They were men he could not control and did not seek to control.

The committee's report, undoubtedly far bolder than

Fear of Communism Stymied Civil Rights

In this excerpt from his book Black Civil Rights in America, *Kevern Verney argues that the rise of anti-communist forces in the late 1940s thwarted civil rights advances. According to Verney, criticism of American race relations was considered subversive.*

In the immediate postwar years civil rights leaders in America sought to use the UN as an international forum to embarrass the federal government over the treatment of its black population. On 6 June 1946, the National Negro Congress (NNC) presented the UN with 'A Petition on Behalf of Thirteen Million Oppressed Negro Citizens of the United States of America'. Even the more conservative NAACP put forward 'An Appeal to the World: A Statement of the Denial of Human Rights of Minorities in the Case of Citizens of Negro Descent in the United States of America, and an Appeal to the United Nations for Redress'.

By the end of the 1940s, however, the prevailing mood of anti-communism made such initiatives all but impossible. Public criticism of race relations in the United States was increasingly seen as unpatriotic and the product of Soviet agitation. . . .

Mainstream civil rights groups and leaders, like Walter White and the National Association for the Advancement of Colored People (NAACP), often sided with the forces of repression in the McCarthy years. In 1948 the Executive Committee and Annual Convention of the Congress of Racial

Truman's expectations, confirmed charges that America treated its Negroes as second-class citizens. It called for FEPC, an antilynching law, an anti-poll tax measure, abolition of segregation in interstate transportation, and the end of discrimination and segregation in federal agencies and the military. By attacking Jim Crow, the committee

Equality (CORE) passed anti-communist resolutions repudiating all links with communist-infiltrated organizations. Individual CORE branches, or chapters, were ordered to cease contact with communists or themselves face expulsion. In 1950 the NAACP launched its own internal investigation of suspected communist sympathizers and the NAACP Board of Directors were authorized to expel individual members or even whole branches. . . .

In one sense the anti-communist purges of the late 1940s and early 1950s helped civil rights groups to regain self-autonomy, reversing the communist entry-ism of the 1930s. In demonstrating their loyalty and patriotism civil rights leaders also hoped to earn the sympathy of politicians and to avoid civil rights being labelled a subversive issue. In the event this expectation proved over-optimistic. Southern national and state leaders were all too successful in using anti-communism as a justification for the official persecution and oppression of civil rights groups. . . .

Taken as a whole, although the anti-communism of the late Truman and early Eisenhower years brought some limited pluses to the cause of black civil rights, these were more than offset by the minuses. The domestic impact of the Cold War, more than any other single factor, helps to explain why the civil rights movement in its most widely recognized form did not emerge until the mid-1950s rather than in the late 1940s.

Kevern Verney, *Black Civil Rights in America*, 2000.

had moved to a redefinition of equality and interpreted segregation as incompatible with equality.

Forced by the report to take a position, he no longer could easily remain an ally of Southern Democrats and maintain the wary allegiance of Negro leaders and urban liberals. Compelled earlier to yield to demands for advancement of the Negro, pressures which he did not wish fully to resist, Truman had encouraged these forces and they were moving beyond his control. On his decision, his political future might precariously rest. Threatened by Henry Wallace's candidacy on a third-party ticket, Truman had to take a bold position on civil rights or risk losing the important votes of urban Negroes. Though he might antagonize Southern voters, he foresaw no risk of losing Southern Democrats, no possibility of a bolt by dissidents, and the mild Southern response to the Civil Rights Report seemed to confirm this judgment.

A Strategy of Moderation

On February 2, 1948, Truman asked the Congress to enact most of the recommendations of his Civil Rights Committee (except most of those attacking segregation). Rather than using his executive powers, as the committee had urged, to end segregation in federal employment or to abolish segregation and discrimination in the military, he *promised* only to issue orders ending discrimination (but not specifying segregation) in the military and in federal agencies. Retreating to moderation, the administration did not submit any of the legislation, nor did Truman issue the promised executive orders. "The strategy," an assistant later explained, "was to start with a bold measure and then temporize to pick up the right-wing forces. Simply stated, backtrack after the bang."

Truman sought to ease Southern doubts by inserting in the 1948 platform the party's moderate 1944 plank on civil rights. Most Negro leaders, fearing the taint of Wallace and unwilling to return to the GOP, appeared stuck with Truman and they praised him. Though they desired a stronger plank, they would not abandon him at the convention, for his advocacy of rights for Negroes was unmatched by any twentieth-century president. To turn their backs on him in this time of need, most Negroes feared, would be injuring their own cause. But others were prepared to struggle for a stronger plank. Urban bosses, persuaded that Truman would lose, hoped to save their local tickets, and prominent white liberals sought power and principle. Triumphing at the convention, they secured a stronger plank, but it did not promise social equality. By promising equality when it was still regarded as compatible with segregation, they were offering far less than the "walk forthrightly into the bright sunshine of human rights," which Hubert Humphrey, then mayor of Minneapolis, had pledged in leading the liberal effort.

When some of the Southerners bolted and formed the States Rights party, Truman was freed of any need for tender courtship of the South. He had to capture the Northern vote. Quickly he issued the long-delayed executive orders, which established a federal antidiscrimination board, declared a policy of equal opportunity in the armed forces, and established a committee to end military discrimination and segregation. (In doing so, Truman courted Negro voters and halted the efforts of A. Philip Randolph to lead a Negro revolt against the draft unless the military was integrated.) Playing politics carefully during the campaign, Truman generally stayed away from civil rights and concentrated on inflation, public housing, and Taft-Hartley.

In the new Democratic Congress Truman could not secure the civil rights program, and a coalition of Southern Democrats and Northern Republicans blocked his efforts. Though liberals were unhappy with his leadership, they did not question his proposed legislation. All agreed on the emphasis on social change through legislation and judicial decisions. The liberal way was the legal way, and it seldom acknowledged the depth of American racism or even considered the possibility of bold new tactics. Only occasionally—in the threatened March on Washington in 1941, in some ride-ins in 1947, and in the campaign of civil disobedience against the draft in 1948—had there been bolder means. In each case Negroes had devised and carried out these tactics. But generally they relied upon more traditional means: they expected white America to yield to political pressure and subscribe to the dictates of American democracy. By relying upon legal change, however, and by emphasizing measures to restore a *modicum* of human dignity, Negroes and whites did not confront the deeper problems of race relations which they failed to understand.

Struggling for moderate institutional changes, liberals were disappointed by Truman's frequent unwillingness to use his executive powers in behalf of the cause he claimed to espouse. Only after considerable pressure did he create a FEPC-type agency during the Korean War. His loyalty-and-security program, in its operation, discriminated against Negroes, and federal investigators, despite protests to Truman, apparently continued to inquire into attitudes of interracial sympathy as evidence relevant to a determination of disloyalty. He was also slow to require the Federal Housing Administration to stop issuing mortgages on property with restrictive covenants, and it continued, by its policies, to protect residential segregation.

Some Civil Rights Achievements

Yet his government was not without significant achievements in civil rights. His special committee had quietly acted to integrate the armed forces, and even the recalcitrant Army had abolished racial quotas when the President secretly promised their restoration if the racial imbalance became severe. And the Department of Justice, despite Truman's apparent indifference, had been an active warrior in the battle against Jim Crow. Entering cases as an *amicus curiae*, Justice had submitted briefs arguing the unconstitutionality of enforcing restrictive covenants and of requiring separate-but-equal facilities in interstate transportation and in higher education. During the summer of 1952, the Solicitor-General's Office even won the administration's approval for a brief directly challenging segregated primary education.

The accomplishments of the Truman years were moderate, and the shortcomings left the nation with a great burden of unresolved problems. Viewed from the perspective of today, Truman's own views seem unduly mild and his government excessively cautious; viewed even by his own time he was a reluctant liberal, troubled by terror and eager to establish limited equality. He was ahead of public opinion in his legislative requests, but not usually in his actions. By his occasional advocacy, he educated the nation and held high the promise of equality. By kindling hope, he also may have prevented rebellion and restrained or delayed impulses to work outside of the system. But he also unleashed expectations he could not foresee, and forces which future governments would not be able to restrain.

APPENDIX OF DOCUMENTS

Document 1: Announcing the Bombing of Hiroshima

On August 6, 1945, the United States dropped an atomic bomb on Hiroshima, Japan. In the following statements, made on August 6 and August 9, President Truman announces that decision, details additional American strategy, and explains why the United States decided to produce and use the bomb.

August 6, 1945: The Bomb Is Dropped

Sixteen hours ago an American airplane dropped one bomb on Hiroshima, an important Japanese Army base. That bomb had more power than 20,000 tons of T.N.T. It had more than two thousand times the blast power of the British "Grand Slam" which is the largest bomb ever yet used in the history of warfare.

The Japanese began the war from the air at Pearl Harbor. They have been repaid many fold. And the end is not yet. With this bomb we have now added a new and revolutionary increase in destruction to supplement the growing power of our armed forces. In their present form these bombs are now in production and even more powerful forms are in development.

It is an atomic bomb. It is a harnessing of the basic power of the universe. The force from which the sun draws its power has been loosed against those who brought war to the Far East. . . .

We are now prepared to obliterate more rapidly and completely every productive enterprise the Japanese have above ground in any city. We shall destroy their docks, their factories, and their communications. Let there be no mistake; we shall completely destroy Japan's power to make war.

It was to spare the Japanese people from utter destruction that the ultimatum of July 26 was issued at Potsdam. Their leaders promptly rejected that ultimatum. If they do not now accept our terms they may expect a rain of ruin from the air, the like of which has never been seen on this earth. Behind this air attack will follow sea and land forces in such numbers and power as they have not yet seen and with the fighting skill of which they are already well aware. . . .

Another Warning (August 9, 1945)

The world will note that the first atomic bomb was dropped on Hiroshima, a military base. That was because we wished in this first attack to avoid, insofar as possible, the killing of civilians. But that attack is only a warning of things to come. If Japan does not surrender, bombs will have to be dropped on her war industries and, unfortunately, thousands of civilian lives will be lost. I urge Japanese civilians to leave industrial cities immediately, and save themselves from destruction.

I realize the tragic significance of the atomic bomb.

Its production and its use were not lightly undertaken by this Government. But we knew that our enemies were on the search for it. We know now how close they were to finding it. And we knew the disaster which would come to this Nation, and to all peace-loving nations, to all civilization, if they had found it first.

That is why we felt compelled to undertake the long and uncertain and costly labor of discovery and production.

We won the race of discovery against the Germans.

Having found the bomb we have used it. We have used it against those who attacked us without warning at Pearl Harbor, against those who have starved and beaten and executed American prisoners of war, against those who have abandoned all pretense of obeying international laws of warfare. We have used it in order to shorten the agony of war, in order to save the lives of thousands and thousands of young Americans.

We shall continue to use it until we completely destroy Japan's power to make war. Only a Japanese surrender will stop us.

Harry Truman, statements from August 6, 1945 and August 9, 1945.

Document 2: Establishing a Peacetime Economy

In his September 1945 twenty-one-point message to Congress, President Truman explains that with World War II over, the American economy needs to reconvert to a peacetime status. He suggests that raising the minimum wage is one step that must be taken.

On May 28, 1945, I recommended to the Congress that the Federal Government immediately supplement the unemployment insurance benefits now provided by the several States. That is the only feasible way to provide at least a subsistence payment in all parts of the United States during this coming unemployment period.

As I pointed out then, the existing State laws relative to unemployment insurance are inadequate in three respects:

(1) Only about 30,000,000 of our 43,000,000 nonagricultural workers are protected by unemployment insurance. Federal Government employees, for example, such as Federal shipyard and arsenal workers, are not covered. Nor are employees of small businesses and small industrial establishments. Nor are the officers and men of the merchant marine who have braved enemy torpedoes and bombs to deliver supplies and the implements of war to our armed services and our allies.

(2) The weekly benefit payments under many of the State laws are now far too low to provide subsistence and purchasing power for the workers and their families. Almost half of the States have the clearly inadequate maximum of $15 to $18 a week.

(3) Many of the States pay benefits for too short a period. In more than one-third of the States, for example, 18 weeks is the maximum.

I recommended then, and I urgently renew my recommendation now, that the Congress take immediate action to make good these deficiencies for the present emergency period of reconversion. . . .

The foundations of a healthy national economy cannot be secure so long as any large section of our working people receive substandard wages. The existence of substandard wage levels sharply curtails the national purchasing power and narrows the market for the products of our farms and factories.

In the Fair Labor Standards Act of 1938, the Congress adopted a program intended to provide a minimum wage standard for a large number of American workers.

In that statute, the Congress declared it to be our national policy to eliminate, from interstate industry, wage levels detrimental to the maintenance of minimum standards of living. The establishment then of a minimum wage of 25 cents per hour represented a first step toward the realization of that policy. The goal of 40 cents per hour, which under the act was to be made effective by 1945, was actually made fully effective more than a year ago by the voluntary action of the industry committees.

I believed that the goal of a 40 cent minimum was inadequate when established. It has now become obsolete.

Increases in the cost of living since 1938 and changes in our national wage structure, require an immediate and substantial upward revision of this minimum. Only in that way can the objectives of the Fair Labor Standards Act be realized, the national purchasing power protected, and an economy of full production and abundance preserved and maintained for the American people.

The high prosperity which we seek in the postwar years will not be meaningful for all our people if any large proportion of our industrial wage earners receive wages as low as the minimum now sanctioned by the Fair Labor Standards Act.

I therefore recommend that the Congress amend the Fair Labor Standards Act by substantially increasing the minimum wage specified therein to a level which will eliminate substandards of living, and assure the maintenance of the health, efficiency, and general well-being of workers. . . .

I am confident that, with the cooperation of American industry, labor, and agriculture, we can bridge the gap between war and peace.

When we have reconverted our economy to a peacetime basis, however, we shall not be satisfied with merely our prewar economy. The American people have set high goals for their own future. They have set these goals high because they have seen how great can be the productive capacity of our country.

The levels of production and income reached during the war years have given our citizens an appreciation of what a full production peacetime economy can be.

They are not interested in boom prosperity—for that only too often leads to panic and depression. But they are interested in providing opportunity for work and for ultimate security.

Government must do its part and assist industry and labor to get over the line from war to peace.

Excerpts from Harry Truman's message to Congress, September 6, 1945.

Document 3: The Truman Doctrine

Following World War II, communism posed a threat to Central and Western Europe. In a 1947 address to Congress, excerpted here, President Truman states that the United States must aid Greece, Turkey, and other nations in order to ensure that those countries will develop peacefully and democratically. The U.S. policy of working to contain the spread of communism in Europe became known as the Truman Doctrine.

The United States has received from the Greek Government an urgent appeal for financial and economic assistance. Preliminary reports from the American economic mission now in Greece and reports from the American Ambassador in Greece corroborate the statement of the Greek Government that assistance is imperative if Greece is to survive as a free nation.

I do not believe that the American people and the Congress wish to turn a deaf ear to the appeal of the Greek Government. . . .

Greece is today without funds to finance the importation of those goods which are essential to bare subsistence. Under these circumstances the people of Greece cannot make progress in solving their problems of reconstruction. Greece is in desperate need of financial and economic assistance to enable it to resume purchases of food, clothing, fuel, and seeds. These are indispensable for the subsistence of its people and are obtainable only from abroad. Greece must have help to import the goods necessary to restore internal order and security so essential for economic and political recovery. . . .

The very existence of the Greek state is today threatened by the terrorist activities of several thousand armed men, led by Communists, who defy the Government's authority at a number of points, particularly along the northern boundaries. A commission appointed by the United Nations Security Council is at present investigating disturbed conditions in northern Greece and alleged border violations along the frontier between Greece on the one hand and Albania, Bulgaria, and Yugoslavia on the other.

Meanwhile, the Greek Government is unable to cope with the situation. The Greek Army is small and poorly equipped. It needs supplies and equipment if it is to restore the authority of the Government throughout Greek territory.

Greece must have assistance if it is to become a self-supporting and self-respecting democracy.

The United States must supply this assistance. We have already extended to Greece certain types of relief and economic aid but these are inadequate.

There is no other country to which democratic Greece can turn.

No other nation is willing and able to provide the necessary support for a democratic Greek Government.

The British Government, which has been helping Greece, can give no further financial or economic aid after March 31. Great Britain finds itself under the necessity of reducing or liquidating its commitments in several parts of the world, including Greece.

We have considered how the United Nations might assist in this crisis. But the situation is an urgent one requiring immediate action, and the United Nations and its related organizations are not in a position to extend help of the kind that is required. . . .

Greece's neighbor, Turkey, also deserves our attention.

The future of Turkey as an independent and economically sound state is clearly no less important to the freedom-loving peoples of the world than the future of Greece. The circumstances in which Turkey finds itself today are considerably different from those of Greece. Turkey has been spared the disasters that have beset Greece. And during the war, the United States and Great Britain furnished Turkey with material aid.

Nevertheless, Turkey now needs our support.

Since the war, Turkey has sought financial assistance from Great Britain and the United States for the purpose of effecting that modernization necessary for the maintenance of its national integrity.

That integrity is essential to the preservation of order in the Middle East.

The British Government has informed us that, owing to its own difficulties, it can no longer extend financial or economic aid to Turkey.

As in the case of Greece, if Turkey is to have the assistance it needs, the United States must supply it. We are the only country able to provide that help.

I am fully aware of the broad implications involved if the United States extends assistance to Greece and Turkey, and I shall discuss these implications with you at this time.

One of the primary objectives of the foreign policy of the United States is the creation of conditions in which we and other nations will be able to work out a way of life free from coercion. This was a fundamental issue in the war with Germany and Japan. Our victory was won over countries which sought to impose their will, and their way of life, upon other nations.

To insure the peaceful development of nations, free from coercion, the United States has taken a leading part in establishing the

United Nations. The United Nations is designed to make possible lasting freedom and independence for all its members. We shall not realize our objectives, however, unless we are willing to help free peoples to maintain their free institutions and their national integrity against aggressive movements that seek to impose upon them totalitarian regimes. This is no more than a frank recognition that totalitarian regimes imposed on free peoples, by direct or indirect aggression, undermine the foundations of international peace and hence the security of the United States.

The peoples of a number of countries of the world have recently had totalitarian regimes forced upon them against their will. The Government of the United States has made frequent protests against coercion and intimidation, in violation of the Yalta agreement, in Poland, Rumania, and Bulgaria. I must also state that in a number of other countries there have been similar developments.

At the present moment in world history nearly every nation must choose between alternative ways of life. The choice is too often not a free one.

One way of life is based upon the will of the majority, and is distinguished by free institutions, representative government, free elections, guarantees of individual liberty, freedom of speech and religion, and freedom from political oppression.

The second way of life is based upon the will of a minority forcibly imposed upon the majority. It relies upon terror and oppression, a controlled press and radio, fixed elections, and the suppression of personal freedoms.

I believe that it must be the policy of the United States to support free peoples who are resisting attempted subjugation by armed minorities or by outside pressures.

I believe that we must assist free peoples to work out their own destinies in their own way.

I believe that our help should be primarily through economic and financial aid, which is essential to economic stability and orderly political processes.

Harry Truman, address before Congress, March 12, 1947.

Document 4: Establishing a Loyalty Program
Concern over the presence of Communists in the American government arose in the 1930s. In the following executive order, issued

March 21, 1947, President Truman outlines procedures to ensure that all government employees are loyal to the United States.

WHEREAS each employee of the Government of the United States is endowed with a measure of trusteeship over the democratic processes which are the heart and sinew of the United States; and

WHEREAS it is of vital importance that persons employed in the Federal service be of complete and unswerving loyalty to the United States; and

WHEREAS, although the loyalty of by far the overwhelming majority of all Government employees is beyond question, the presence within the Government service of any disloyal or subversive person constitutes a threat to our democratic processes; and

WHEREAS maximum protection must be afforded the United States against infiltration of disloyal persons into the ranks of its employees, and equal protection from unfounded accusations of disloyalty must be afforded the loyal employees of the Government: NOW, THEREFORE . . .

PART I—INVESTIGATION OF APPLICANTS

1. There shall be a loyalty investigation of every person entering the civilian employment of any department or agency of the executive branch of the Federal Government. . . .

2. The investigations of persons entering the employ of the executive branch may be conducted after any such person enters upon actual employment therein, but in any such case the appointment of such person shall be conditioned upon a favorable determination with respect to his loyalty. . . .

3. An investigation shall be made of all applicants at all available pertinent sources of information and shall include reference to:

a. Federal Bureau of Investigation files.

b. Civil Service Commission files.

c. Military and naval intelligence files.

d. The files of any other appropriate government investigative or intelligence agency.

e. House Committee on un-American Activities files.

f. Local law-enforcement files at the place of residence and employment of the applicant, including municipal, county, and State law-enforcement files.

g. Schools and colleges attended by applicant.

h. Former employers of applicant.

i. References given by applicant.

j. Any other appropriate source.

4. Whenever derogatory information with respect to loyalty of an applicant is revealed a full field investigation shall be conducted. A full field investigation shall also be conducted of those applicants, or of applicants for particular positions, as may be designated by the head of the employing department or agency, such designations to be based on the determination by any such head of the best interests of national security.

PART II—INVESTIGATION OF EMPLOYEES

1. The head of each department and agency in the executive branch of the Government shall be personally responsible for an effective program to assure that disloyal civilian officers or employees are not retained in employment in his department or agency. . . .

2. The head of each department and agency shall appoint one or more loyalty boards, each composed of not less than three representatives of the department or agency concerned, for the purpose of hearing loyalty cases arising within such department or agency and making recommendations with respect to the removal of any officer or employee of such department or agency on grounds relating to loyalty, and he shall prescribe regulations for the conduct of the proceedings before such boards. . . .

3. A recommendation of removal by a loyalty board shall be subject to appeal by the officer or employee affected, prior to his removal, to the head of the employing department or agency or to such person or persons as may be designated by such head, under such regulations as may be prescribed by him, and the decision of the department or agency concerned shall be subject to appeal to the Civil Service Commission's Loyalty Review Board, hereinafter provided for, for an advisory recommendation.

4. The rights of hearing, notice thereof, and appeal therefrom shall be accorded to every officer or employee prior to his removal on grounds of disloyalty, irrespective of tenure, or of manner, method, or nature of appointment, but the head of the employing department or agency may suspend any officer or employee at any time pending a determination with respect to loyalty.

5. The loyalty boards of the various departments and agencies shall furnish to the Loyalty Review Board, hereinafter provided for,

such reports as may be requested concerning the operation of the loyalty program in any such department or agency.

Harry Truman, excerpts from executive order no. 9835, March 21, 1947.

Document 5: The Marshall Plan

In a June 1947 commencement speech at Harvard University, Secretary of State George C. Marshall outlines the economic troubles of postwar Europe and maintains that the United States must help the continent recover. This speech would form the basis of the European Recovery Program, better known as the Marshall Plan.

I need not tell you gentlemen that the world situation is very serious. That must be apparent to all intelligent people. I think one difficulty is that the problem is one of such enormous complexity that the very mass of facts presented to the public by press and radio make it exceedingly difficult for the man in the street to reach a clear appraisement of the situation. Furthermore, the people of this country are distant from the troubled areas of the earth and it is hard for them to comprehend the plight and consequent reactions of the long-suffering peoples, and the effect of those reactions on their governments in connection with our efforts to promote peace in the world.

In considering the requirements for the rehabilitation of Europe, the physical loss of life, the visible destruction of cities, factories, mines, and railroads was correctly estimated, but it has become obvious during recent months that this visible destruction was probably less serious than the dislocation of the entire fabric of European economy. For the past 10 years conditions have been highly abnormal. The feverish preparation for war and the more feverish maintenance of the war effort engulfed all aspects of national economies. Machinery has fallen into disrepair or is entirely obsolete. Under the arbitrary and destructive Nazi rule, virtually every possible enterprise was geared into the German war machine. Long-standing commercial ties, private institutions, banks, insurance companies and shipping companies disappeared through loss of capital, absorption through nationalization or by simple destruction. In many countries, confidence in the local currency has been severely shaken. The breakdown of the business structure of Europe during the war was complete. Recovery has been seriously retarded by the fact that 2 years after the close of hostilities a peace settlement with Germany and Austria has not been agreed upon. But even given a more prompt solution of these difficult problems, the rehabilitation of the economic structure of Europe quite evidently will require a much longer time and greater effort than had been foreseen.

There is a phase of this matter which is both interesting and serious. The farmer has always produced the foodstuffs to exchange with the city dweller for the other necessities of life. This division of labor is the basis of modern civilization. At the present time it is threatened with breakdown. The town and city industries are not producing adequate goods to exchange with the food-producing farmer. Raw materials and fuel are in short supply. Machinery is lacking or worn out. The farmer or the peasant cannot find the goods for sale which he desires to purchase. So the sale of his farm produce for money which he cannot use seems to him an unprofitable transaction. He, therefore, has withdrawn many fields from crop cultivation and is using them for grazing. He feeds more grain to stock and finds for himself and his family an ample supply of food, however short he may be on clothing and the other ordinary gadgets of civilization. Meanwhile people in the cities are short of food and fuel. So the governments are forced to use their foreign money and credits to procure these necessities abroad. This process exhausts funds which are urgently needed for reconstruction. Thus a very serious situation is rapidly developing which bodes no good for the world. The modern system of the division of labor upon which the exchange of products is based is in danger of breaking down.

The truth of the matter is that Europe's requirements for the next 3 or 4 years of foreign food and other essential products—principally from America—are so much greater than her present ability to pay that she must have substantial additional help, or face economic, social, and political deterioration of a very grave character.

Restoring European Confidence

The remedy lies in breaking the vicious circle and restoring the confidence of the European people in the economic future of their own countries and of Europe as a whole. The manufacturer and the farmer throughout wide areas must be able and willing to exchange their products for currencies the continuing value of which is not open to question.

Aside from the demoralizing effect on the world at large and the possibilities of disturbances arising as a result of the desperation of the people concerned, the consequences to the economy of the United States should be apparent to all. It is logical that the United States should do whatever it is able to do to assist in the return of normal economic health in the world, without which there can be no political stability and no assured peace. Our policy is directed not against any country or doctrine but against hunger, poverty, desperation, and chaos. Its purpose should be the revival of a working economy in the world so as to permit the emergence of political and social conditions in which free institutions can exist. Such assistance, I am convinced, must not be on a piecemeal basis as various crises develop. Any assistance that this Government may render in the future should provide a cure rather than a mere palliative. Any government that is willing to assist in the task of recovery will find full cooperation, I am sure, on the part of the United States Government. Any government which maneuvers to block the recovery of other countries cannot expect help from us. Furthermore, governments, political parties, or groups which seek to perpetuate human misery in order to profit therefrom politically or otherwise will encounter the opposition of the United States.

It is already evident that, before the United States Government can proceed much further in its efforts to alleviate the situation and help start the European world on its way to recovery, there must be some agreement among the countries of Europe as to the requirements of the situation and the part those countries themselves will take in order to give proper effect to whatever action might be undertaken by this Government. It would be neither fitting nor efficacious for this Government to undertake to draw up unilaterally a program designed to place Europe on its feet economically. This is the business of the Europeans. The initiative, I think, must come from Europe. The role of this country should consist of friendly aid in the drafting of a European program and of later support of such a program so far as it may be practical for us to do so. The program should be a joint one, agreed to by a number, if not all European nations.

An essential part of any successful action on the part of the United States is an understanding on the part of the people of America of the character of the problem and the remedies to be applied. Political passion and prejudice should have no part. With foresight, and a willingness on the part of our people to face up to the vast responsibility which history has clearly placed upon our country, the difficulties I have outlined can and will be overcome.

George C. Marshall, speech at Harvard University, June 5, 1947.

Document 6: The Taft-Hartley Veto

In 1947, Congress passed the Taft-Hartley bill, which placed restrictions on labor unions. President Truman vetoed the bill, arguing that it would cause workers to lose protections they currently held. Congress, however, overturned the veto.

I find that this bill is completely contrary to that national policy of economic freedom. It would require the Government, in effect, to become an unwanted participant at every bargaining table. It would establish by law limitations on the terms of every bargaining agreement, and nullify thousands of agreements mutually arrived at and satisfactory to the parties. It would inject the Government deeply into the process by which employers and workers reach agreement. It would superimpose bureaucratic procedures on the free decisions of local employers and employees. . . .

The bill would deprive workers of vital protection which they now have under the law.

(1) The bill would make it easier for an employer to get rid of employees whom he wanted to discharge because they exercised their right of self-organization guaranteed by the act. It would permit an employer to dismiss a man on the pretext of a slight infraction of shop rules, even though his real motive was to discriminate against this employee for union activity.

(2) The bill would also put a powerful new weapon in the hands of employers by permitting them to initiate elections at times strategically advantageous to them. It is significant that employees on economic strike who may have been replaced are denied a vote. An employer could easily thwart the will of his employees by raising a question of representation at a time when the union was striking over contract terms.

(3) It would give employers the means to engage in endless litigation, draining the energy and resources of unions in court actions, even though the particular charges were groundless.

(4) It would deprive workers of the power to meet the competi-

tion of goods produced under sweatshop conditions by permitting employers to halt every type of secondary boycott, not merely those for unjustifiable purposes.

(5) It would reduce the responsibility of employers for unfair labor practices committed in their behalf. The effect of the bill is to narrow unfairly employer liability for antiunion acts and statements made by persons who, in the eyes of the employees affected, act and speak for management, but who may not be "agents" in the strict legal sense of that term.

(6) At the same time it would expose unions to suits for acts of violence, wildcat strikes and other actions, none of which were authorized or ratified by them. By employing elaborate legal doctrine, the bill applies a superficially similar test of responsibility for employers and unions—each would be responsible for the acts of his "agents." But the power of an employer to control the acts of his subordinates is direct and final. This is radically different from the power of unions to control the acts of their members—who are, after all, members of a free association. . . .

The most fundamental test which I have applied to this bill is whether it would strengthen or weaken American democracy in the present critical hour. This bill is perhaps the most serious economic and social legislation of the past decade. Its effects—for good or ill—would be felt for decades to come.

I have concluded that the bill is a clear threat to the successful working of our democratic society.

One of the major lessons of recent world history is that free and vital trade unions are a strong bulwark against the growth of totalitarian movements. We must, therefore, be everlastingly alert that in striking at union abuses we do not destroy the contribution which unions make to our democratic strength.

This bill would go far toward weakening our trade-union movement. And it would go far toward destroying our national unity. By raising barriers between labor and management and by injecting political considerations into normal economic decisions, it would invite them to gain their ends through direct political action. I think it would be exceedingly dangerous to our country to develop a class basis for political action.

Harry Truman, excerpts from veto message, June 20, 1947.

Document 7: Separate and Not Equal

President Truman formed a committee in December 1946 to study the issues of civil rights and discrimination. In October 1947 the President's Committee on Civil Rights released a report titled To Secure These Rights, *which is excerpted below. Among the issues covered in the report was the lack of educational opportunities for African Americans.*

The United States has made remarkable progress toward the goal of universal education for its people. The number and variety of its schools and colleges are greater than ever before. Student bodies have become increasingly representative of all the different peoples who make up our population. Yet we have not finally eliminated prejudice and discrimination from the operation of either our public or our private schools and colleges. Two inadequacies are extremely serious. We have failed to provide Negroes and, to a lesser extent, other minority group members with equality of educational opportunities in our public institutions, particularly at the elementary and secondary school levels. We have allowed discrimination in the operation of many of our private institutions of higher education, particularly in the North with respect to Jewish students.

Discrimination in public schools.—The failure to give Negroes equal educational opportunities is naturally most acute in the South, where approximately 10 million Negroes live. The South is one of the poorer sections of the country and has at best only limited funds to spend on its schools. With 34.5 percent of the country's population, 17 southern states and the District of Columbia have 39.4 percent of our school children. Yet the South has only one-fifth of the taxpaying wealth of the nation. Actually, on a percentage basis, the South spends a greater share of its income on education than do the wealthier states in other parts of the country. For example, Mississippi, which has the lowest expenditure per school child of any state, is ninth in percentage of income devoted to education. A recent study showed Mississippi spending 3.41 percent of its income for education as against New York's figure of only 2.61 percent. But this meant $400 per classroom unit in Mississippi, and $4,100 in New York. Negro and white school children both suffer because of the South's basic inability to match the level of educational opportunity provided in other sections of the nation.

But it is the South's segregated school system which most directly discriminates against the Negro. This segregation is found today in 17 southern states and the District of Columbia. Poverty-stricken though it was after the close of the Civil War, the South chose to maintain two sets of public schools, one for whites and one for Negroes. With respect to education, as well as to other public services, the Committee believes that the "separate but equal" rule has not been obeyed in practice. There is a marked difference in quality between the educational opportunities offered white children and Negro children in the separate schools.

President's Committee on Civil Rights, *To Secure These Rights*, October 1947.

Document 8: A Call to Enforce Civil Rights

Civil rights became a national political issue during Truman's presidency. In a special message, issued February 2, 1948, President Truman tells Congress that it should pass legislation that will protect the right of minorities to vote, take action against lynching, and prevent employment discrimination.

In the State of the Union Message on January 7, 1948, I spoke of five great goals toward which we should strive in our constant effort to strengthen our democracy and improve the welfare of our people. The first of these is to secure fully our essential human rights. I am now presenting to the Congress my recommendations for legislation to carry us forward toward that goal.

This Nation was founded by men and women who sought these shores that they might enjoy greater freedom and greater opportunity than they had known before. The founders of the United States proclaimed to the world the American belief that all men are created equal, and that governments are instituted to secure the inalienable rights with which all men are endowed. In the Declaration of Independence and the Constitution of the United States, they eloquently expressed the aspirations of . . . mankind for equality and freedom. . . .

We believe that all men are created equal and that they have the right to equal justice under law.

We believe that all men have the right to freedom of thought and of expression and the right to worship as they please.

We believe that all men are entitled to equal opportunities for jobs, for homes, for good health and for education.

We believe that all men should have a voice in their government and that government should protect, not usurp, the rights of the people.

These are the basic civil rights which are the source and the support of our democracy.

Today, the American people enjoy more freedom and opportunity than ever before. Never in our history has there been better reason to hope for the complete realization of the ideals of liberty and equality. . . .

The Federal Government has a clear duty to see that Constitutional guarantees of individual liberties and of equal protection under the laws are not denied or abridged anywhere in our Union. That duty is shared by all three branches of the Government, but it can be fulfilled only if the Congress enacts modern, comprehensive civil rights laws, adequate to the needs of the day, and demonstrating our continuing faith in the free way of life. . . .

Strengthening the Government Organization

As a first step, we must strengthen the organization of the Federal Government in order to enforce civil rights legislation more adequately and to watch over the state of our traditional liberties.

I recommend that the Congress establish a permanent Commission on Civil Rights reporting to the President. The Commission should continuously review our civil rights policies and practices, study specific problems, and make recommendations to the President at frequent intervals. It should work with other agencies of the Federal Government, with state and local governments, and with private organizations.

I also suggest that the Congress establish a joint Congressional Committee on Civil Rights. This Committee should make a continuing study of legislative matters relating to civil rights and should consider means of improving respect for and enforcement of those rights. . . .

A specific Federal measure is needed to deal with the crime of lynching—against which I cannot speak too strongly. It is a principle of our democracy, written into our Constitution, that every person accused of an offense against the law shall have a fair, orderly trial in an impartial court. We have made great progress toward this end, but I regret to say that lynching has not yet finally disappeared from our land. So long as one person walks in fear of lynching, we shall not have achieved equal justice under law. I call upon the Congress to take decisive action against this crime.

Protecting the Right to Vote

Under the Constitution, the right of all properly qualified citizens to vote is beyond question. Yet the exercise of this right is still subject to interference. Some individuals are prevented from voting by isolated acts of intimidation. Some whole groups are prevented by outmoded policies prevailing in certain states or communities.

We need stronger statutory protection of the right to vote. I urge the Congress to enact legislation forbidding interference by public officers or private persons with the right of qualified citizens to participate in primary, special and general elections in which Federal officers are to be chosen. This legislation should extend to elections for state as well as Federal officers insofar as interference with the right to vote results from discriminatory action by public officers based on race, color, or other unreasonable classification.

Requirements for the payment of poll taxes also interfere with the right to vote. There are still seven states which, by their constitutions, place this barrier between their citizens and the ballot box. The American people would welcome voluntary action on the part of these states to remove this barrier. Nevertheless, I believe the Congress should enact measures insuring that the right to vote in elections for Federal officers shall not be contingent upon the payment of taxes.

I wish to make it clear that the enactment of the measures I have recommended will in no sense result in Federal conduct of elections. They are designed to give qualified citizens Federal protection of their right to vote. The actual conduct of elections, as always, will remain the responsibility of State governments.

Fair Employment Practice Commission

We in the United States believe that all men are entitled to equality of opportunity. Racial, religious and other invidious forms of discrimination deprive the individual of an equal chance to develop and utilize his talents and to enjoy the rewards of his efforts.

Once more I repeat my request that the Congress enact fair employment practice legislation prohibiting discrimination in employment based on race, color, religion or national origin. The legislation should create a Fair Employment Practice Commission with authority to prevent discrimination by employers and labor unions, trade and professional associations, and government agencies and employment bureaus. The degree of effectiveness which the wartime Fair Employment Practice Committee attained shows that it is possible to equalize job opportunity by government action and thus to eliminate the influence of prejudice in employment.

Harry Truman, message to Congress, February 2, 1948.

Document 9: Desegregating the Armed Forces

On July 26, 1948, President Truman issued an executive order announcing the end of segregation of all branches of the armed forces and the establishment of a committee to carry out the policy.

WHEREAS it is essential that there be maintained in the armed services of the United States the highest standards of democracy, with equality of treatment and opportunity for all those who serve in our country's defense:

NOW, THEREFORE, by virtue of the authority vested in me as President of the United States, by the Constitution and the statutes of the United States, and as Commander in Chief of the armed services, it is hereby ordered as follows:

1. It is hereby declared to be the policy of the President that there shall be equality of treatment and opportunity for all persons in the armed services without regard to race, color, religion or national origin. This policy shall be put into effect as rapidly as possible, having due regard to the time required to effectuate any necessary changes without impairing efficiency or morale.

2. There shall be created in the National Military Establishment an advisory committee to be known as the President's Committee on Equality of Treatment and Opportunity in the Armed Services, which shall be composed of seven members to be designated by the President.

3. The Committee is authorized on behalf of the President to examine into the rules, procedures and practices of the armed services in order to determine in what respect such rules, procedures and practices may be altered or improved with a view to carrying out the policy of this order. The Committee shall confer and advise with the Secretary of Defense, the Secretary of the Army, the Secretary of the Navy, and the Secretary of the Air Force, and shall make such recommendations to the President and to said Secretaries as

in the judgment of the Committee will effectuate the policy hereof.

4. All executive departments and agencies of the Federal Government are authorized and directed to cooperate with the Committee in its work, and to furnish the Committee such information or the services of such persons as the Committee may require in the performance of its duties.

Harry Truman, executive order no. 9981, July 26, 1948.

Document 10: Sending Troops to South Korea

On June 25, 1950, North Korean armies invaded South Korea. Two days later, President Truman announced that he had ordered American air and sea forces to South Korea. In the portion of that speech excerpted below, the president explains why he believes U.S. intervention in Korea is necessary.

In Korea the Government forces, which were armed to prevent border raids and to preserve internal security, were attacked by invading forces from North Korea. The Security Council of the United Nations called upon the invading troops to cease hostilities and to withdraw to the thirty-eighth parallel. This they have not done, but on the contrary have pressed the attack. The Security Council called upon all members of the United Nations to render every assistance to the United Nations in the execution of this resolution. In these circumstances I have ordered United States air and sea forces to give the Korean Government troops cover and support.

The attack upon Korea makes it plain beyond all doubt that communism has passed beyond the use of subversion to conquer independent nations and will now use armed invasion and war. It has defied the orders of the Security Council of the United Nations issued to preserve international peace and security. In these circumstances the occupation of Formosa by Communist forces would be a direct threat to the security of the Pacific area and to United States forces performing their lawful and necessary functions in that area.

Accordingly I have ordered the Seventh Fleet to prevent any attack on Formosa. As a corollary of this action I am calling upon the Chinese Government on Formosa to cease all air and sea operations against the mainland. The Seventh Fleet will see that this is done. The determination of the future status of Formosa must await the restoration of security in the Pacific, a peace settlement with Japan, or consideration by the United Nations.

I have also directed that United States forces in the Philippines be strengthened and that military assistance to the Philippine Government be accelerated.

I have similarly directed acceleration in the furnishing of military assistance to the forces of France and the associated states in Indochina and the dispatch of a military mission to provide close working relations with those forces.

I know that all members of the United Nations will consider carefully the consequences of this latest aggression in Korea in defiance of the Charter of the United Nations. A return to the rule of force in international affairs would have far-reaching effects. The United States will continue to uphold the rule of Law.

I have instructed Ambassador Austin, as the representative of the United States to the Security Council, to report these steps to the Council.

Harry Truman, statement on June 27, 1950.

Document 11: Veto of the Internal Security Act

The Internal Security Act, passed by Congress in September 1950, required all Communist organizations to register with the attorney general and placed employment and travel restrictions on Communists. In his veto of the bill, President Truman writes that the act is impractical and threatens freedom of expression. His veto was overturned.

I return herewith, without my approval, H.R. 9490, the proposed "Internal Security Act of 1950."

I am taking this action only after the most serious study and reflection and after consultation with the security and intelligence agencies of the Government. The Department of Justice, the Department of Defense, the Central Intelligence Agency, and the Department of State have all advised me that the bill would seriously damage the security and intelligence operations for which they are responsible. They have strongly expressed the hope that the bill would not become law. . . .

H.R. 9490 would not hurt the Communists. Instead, it would help them. . . .

In brief, when all the provisions of H.R. 9490 are considered together, it is evident that the great bulk of them are not directed toward the real and present dangers that exist from communism. Instead of striking blows at communism, they would strike blows at our own liberties and at our position in the forefront of those working for freedom in the world. . . .

Most of the first 17 sections of H.R. 9490 are concerned with requiring registration and annual reports. . . .

The idea of requiring Communist organizations to divulge information about themselves is a simple and attractive one. But it is about as practical as requiring thieves to register with the sheriff. Obviously, no such organization as the Communist Party is likely to register voluntarily. . . .

A Threat to the Freedoms of Speech, Press, and Assembly
Insofar as the bill would require registration by the Communist Party itself, it does not endanger our traditional liberties. However, the application of the registration requirements to so-called Communist-front organizations can be the greatest danger to freedom of speech, press, and assembly, since the Alien and Sedition Laws of 1798. This danger arises out of the criteria or standards to be applied in determining whether an organization is a Communist-front organization.

There would be no serious problem if the bill required proof that an organization was controlled and financed by the Communist Party before it could be classified as a Communist-front organization. However, recognizing the difficulty of proving those matters, the bill would permit such a determination to be based solely upon the extent to which the positions taken or advanced by it from time to time on matters of policy do not deviate from those of the Communist movement.

This provision could easily be used to classify as a Communist-front organization any organization which is advocating a single policy or objective which is also being urged by the Communist Party or by a Communist foreign government. In fact, this may be the intended result, since the bill defines "organization" to include "a group of persons permanently or temporarily associated together for joint action on any subject or subjects." Thus, an organization which advocates low-cost housing for sincere humanitarian reasons might be classified as a Communist-front organization because the Communists regularly exploit slum conditions as one of their fifth-column techniques.

It is not enough to say that this probably would not be done. The mere fact that it could be done shows clearly how the bill would open a Pandora's box of opportunities for official condemnation of organizations and individuals for perfectly honest opinions which happen to be stated also by Communists.

Suppressing Opinion and Belief

The basic error of these sections is that they move in the direction of suppressing opinion and belief. This would be a very dangerous course to take, not because we have any sympathy for Communist opinions, but because any governmental stifling of the free expression of opinion is a long step toward totalitarianism.

There is no more fundamental axiom of American freedom than the familiar statement: In a free country, we punish men for the crimes they commit, but never for the opinions they have. . . .

We can and we will prevent espionage, sabotage, or other actions endangering our national security. But we would betray our finest traditions if we attempted, as this bill would attempt, to curb the simple expression of opinion. . . .

And what kind of effect would these provisions have on the normal expression of political views? Obviously, if this law were on the statute books, the part of prudence would be to avoid saying anything that might be construed by someone as not deviating sufficiently from the current Communist propaganda line. And since no one could be sure in advance what views were safe to express, the inevitable tendency would be to express no views on controversial subjects.

The result could only be to reduce the vigor and strength of our political life—an outcome that the Communists would happily welcome, but that free men should abhor.

We need not fear the expression of ideas—we do need to fear their suppression.

Our position in the vanguard of freedom rests largely on our demonstration that the free expression of opinion, coupled with government by popular consent, leads to national strength and human advancement. Let us not, in cowering and foolish fear, throw away the ideals which are the fundamental basis of our free society.

Harry Truman, excerpts from veto message, September 22, 1950.

Document 12: A General Is Dismissed

General Douglas MacArthur had been appointed in July 1950 to lead American and U.N. forces in South Korea. However, a conflict with the Truman administration on strategy led to MacArthur's dismissal. In an address to the nation, President Truman explains American policy in Korea and why he decided to relieve MacArthur of his duties.

I want to talk plainly to you tonight about what we are doing in Korea and about our policy in the Far East.

In the simplest terms, what we are doing in Korea is this: We are trying to prevent a third world war.

I think most people in this country recognized that fact last June. And they warmly supported the decision of the Government to help the Republic of Korea against the Communist aggressors. Now, many persons, even some who applauded our decision to defend Korea, have forgotten the basic reason for our action.

It is right for us to be in Korea. It was right last June. It is right today.

I want to remind you why this is true.

The Communists in the Kremlin are engaged in a monstrous conspiracy to stamp out freedom all over the world. If they were to succeed, the United States would be numbered among their principal victims. It must be clear to everyone that the United States cannot—and will not—sit idly by and await foreign conquest. The only question is: When is the best time to meet the threat and how?

The best time to meet the threat is in the beginning. It is easier to put out a fire in the beginning when it is small than after it has become a roaring blaze.

And the best way to meet the threat of aggression is for the peace-loving nations to act together. If they don't act together, they are likely to be picked off, one by one. . . .

We do not want to see the conflict in Korea extended. We are trying to prevent a world war—not to start one. The best way to do that is to make it plain that we and the other free countries will continue to resist the attack.

Avoiding the Spread of Conflict

But you may ask: Why can't we take other steps to punish the aggressor? Why don't we bomb Manchuria and China itself? Why don't we assist Chinese Nationalist troops to land on the mainland of China?

If we were to do these things we would be running a very grave risk of starting a general war. If that were to happen, we would have brought about the exact situation we are trying to prevent. If we were to do these things, we would become entangled in a vast conflict on the continent of Asia and our task would become immeasurably more difficult all over the world.

What would suit the ambitions of the Kremlin better than for our military forces to be committed to a full-scale war with Red China?

It may well be that, in spite of our best efforts, the Communists may spread the war. But it would be wrong—tragically wrong—for us to take the initiative in extending the war.

The dangers are great. Make no mistake about it. Behind the North Koreans and Chinese Communists in the front lines stand additional millions of Chinese soldiers. And behind the Chinese stand the tanks, the planes, the submarines, the soldiers, and the scheming rulers of the Soviet Union.

Our aim is to avoid the spread of the conflict.

The course we have been following is the one best calculated to avoid an all-out war. It is the course consistent with our obligation to do all we can to maintain international peace and security. Our experience in Greece and Berlin shows that it is the most effective course of action we can follow.

First of all, it is clear that our efforts in Korea can blunt the will of the Chinese Communists to continue the struggle. The United Nations forces have put up a tremendous fight in Korea and have inflicted very heavy casualties on the enemy. Our forces are stronger now than they have been before. These are plain facts which may discourage the Chinese Communists from continuing their attack.

Second, the free world as a whole is growing in military strength every day. In the United States, in Western Europe, and throughout the world, free men are alert to the Soviet threat and are building their defenses. This may discourage the Communist rulers from continuing the war in Korea—and from undertaking new acts of aggression elsewhere.

If the Communist authorities realize that they cannot defeat us in Korea, if they realize it would be foolhardy to widen the hostilities beyond Korea, then they may recognize the folly of continuing their aggression. A peaceful settlement may then be possible. The door is always open. Then we may achieve a settlement in Korea which will not compromise the principles and purposes of the United Nations.

MacArthur's Dismissal

I have thought long and hard about this question of extending the war in Asia. I have discussed it many times with the ablest military advisers in the country. I believe with all my heart that the course we are following is the best course.

I believe that we must try to limit the war to Korea for these vital reasons: to make sure that the precious lives of our fighting men are not wasted; to see that the security of our country and the free world is not needlessly jeopardized; and to prevent a third world war.

A number of events have made it evident that General MacArthur did not agree with that policy. I have therefore considered it essential to relieve General MacArthur so that there would be no doubt or confusion as to the real purpose and aim of our policy.

It was with the deepest personal regret that I found myself compelled to take this action. General MacArthur is one of our greatest military commanders. But the cause of world peace is more important than any individual.

The change in commands in the Far East means no change whatever in the policy of the United States. We will carry on the fight in Korea with vigor and determination in an effort to bring the war to a speedy and successful conclusion.

Harry Truman, address to the nation, April 11, 1951.

Chronology

May 8, 1884
Harry S. Truman is born in Lamar, Missouri.

December 1890
The Trumans move to Independence, Missouri.

1890
Truman meets Elizabeth Virginia (Bess) Wallace in Sunday school.

May 1901
Truman graduates from Independence High School.

1906–1917
Truman works on family farm in Grandview, Missouri.

April 6, 1917
The United States enters World War I.

1917–1919
Truman serves in World War I as a captain in the 129th Field Artillery of the 35th Division.

May 6, 1919
Truman receives his Army discharge.

June 28, 1919
Truman weds Bess Wallace; the Treaty of Versailles is signed, ending World War I.

November 7, 1922
Truman is elected Eastern District judge of the Jackson County Court in Missouri.

FEBRUARY 17, 1924
Harry and Bess Truman's only child, Mary Margaret, is born.

NOVEMBER 4, 1924
Truman is defeated for reelection as the Eastern District judge.

NOVEMBER 2, 1926
Truman is elected to the first of two terms as presiding judge of the Jackson County Court.

NOVEMBER 8, 1932
Franklin D. Roosevelt elected to his first of four terms as president of the United States.

AUGUST 7, 1934
Truman wins the Missouri Democratic primary for U.S. Senate.

NOVEMBER 6, 1934
Truman is elected to the U.S. Senate.

1938
Truman helps write the Civil Aeronautics Act, which establishes uniform rules for the aviation industry.

SEPTEMBER 1, 1939
Germany invades Poland, setting off World War II.

1940
Truman helps write the Transportation Act, which provides government oversight of railroad reorganization.

NOVEMBER 5, 1940
Truman is reelected to the Senate.

1941–1945
Truman chairs the Special Committee to Investigate the National Defense Program (better known as the Truman Committee), which studies the awarding of defense contracts.

DECEMBER 7, 1941
The Japanese army bombs Pearl Harbor, prompting the United States to enter World War II.

JULY 21, 1944
Roosevelt nominates Truman to be vice president.

NOVEMBER 7, 1944
Roosevelt and Truman win the presidential election.

APRIL 12, 1945
Roosevelt dies; Truman is sworn in as president.

MAY 8, 1945
Germany surrenders to the Allies, ending World War II in Europe.

JULY 16, 1945
The atomic bomb is successfully tested in Los Alamos, New Mexico.

JULY 28, 1945
The U.S. Senate ratifies the United Nations charter.

AUGUST 6, 1945
The United States drops an atomic bomb on Hiroshima, Japan.

AUGUST 9, 1945
The United States drops an atomic bomb on Nagasaki, Japan.

AUGUST 14, 1945
Japan surrenders to the Allies, ending World War II in Asia.

SEPTEMBER 6, 1945
Truman sends his Twenty-one Point Address to Congress, which contains most of his Fair Deal domestic program.

NOVEMBER 5, 1946
The Republicans win control of the House and Senate.

December 1946
Truman appoints the members of the President's Commission on Civil Rights.

March 12, 1947
Truman delivers his Truman Doctrine speech.

June 5, 1947
In a commencement speech at Harvard University, Secretary of State George C. Marshall outlines what will become the European Recovery Program, better known as the Marshall Plan.

June 20, 1947
Truman vetoes the Taft-Hartley Act. Congress overrides the veto and passes the act, which limits the power of unions by outlawing union-only workplaces, forbidding unions to make contributions to political campaigns, and giving the government the power to place an eighty-day injunction on strikes it deems a threat to national safety.

July 26, 1947
Truman signs the National Security Act of 1947, which unifies the armed forces.

October 29, 1947
Truman receives *To Secure These Rights*, the report prepared by the President's Commission on Civil Rights.

February 2, 1948
Truman submits his civil rights program to Congress.

April 3, 1948
The Marshall Plan is implemented, following Truman's signing of the Foreign Assistance Act.

May 14, 1948
Eleven minutes after it declares its independence, Truman recognizes the state of Israel.

June 24, 1948
The Soviet Union sets up a blockade between Berlin and the West.

June 26, 1948
The United States and Great Britain begin the Berlin airlift, which provides food and other supplies to West Berlin.

July 15, 1948
Truman wins the Democratic nomination for president.

July 26, 1948
Truman issues executive orders directing the end of discrimination in the federal government and armed forces.

November 2, 1948
Truman wins reelection, defeating Thomas Dewey.

April 4, 1949
The North Atlantic Treaty Organization (NATO) is established by the United States, Canada, Belgium, Denmark, France, Great Britain, Iceland, Italy, Luxembourg, the Netherlands, Norway, and Portugal. This treaty provides for collective self-defense, declaring that an armed attack against any member will be treated as an attack against all members.

May 12, 1949
The Soviet Union lifts the Berlin blockade; the Berlin airlift ends.

June 25, 1950
South Korea is invaded by the North Korean People's Army.

June 27, 1950
Truman authorizes the use of American military forces in Korea.

June 30, 1950
Truman commits ground troops to Korea.

JULY 1950
Truman appoints General Douglas MacArthur to be supreme commander of American and UN forces in Korea.

OCTOBER 15, 1950
Truman and MacArthur meet on Wake Island to discuss the Korean War.

APRIL 11, 1951
Truman dismisses General MacArthur.

MARCH 29, 1952
Truman announces he will not run for reelection.

APRIL 8, 1952
Truman announces that he is seizing the steel mills, in order to prevent a strike.

JUNE 2, 1952
The U.S. Supreme Court declares the seizure unconstitutional; a seven-week strike soon follows.

JULY 26, 1952
Adlai Stevenson wins the Democratic nomination of president.

NOVEMBER 4, 1952
Dwight D. Eisenhower defeats Stevenson in the presidential election.

JULY 27, 1953
The Korean War ends.

1955–1956
Truman's two-volume *Memoirs* are published.

JULY 6, 1957
The Truman Library in Independence, Missouri, is dedicated.

DECEMBER 26, 1972
Truman dies in Kansas City, Missouri, at age eighty-eight.

FOR FURTHER RESEARCH

TRUMAN AND HIS POLICIES

WILLIAM C. BERMAN, *The Politics of Civil Rights in the Truman Administration*. Columbus: Ohio State University Press, 1970.

BARTON J. BERNSTEIN, ED., *Politics and Policies of the Truman Administration*. Chicago: Quadrangle Books, 1970.

BARTON J. BERNSTEIN, ED., *Towards a New Past: Dissenting Essays in American History*. New York: Pantheon Books, 1968.

BARTON J. BERNSTEIN AND ALLEN J. MATUSOW, EDS., *The Truman Administration: A Documentary History*. New York: Harper and Row, 1966.

BERT COCHRAN, *Harry Truman and the Crisis Presidency*. New York: Funk and Wagnalls, 1973.

ROBERT J. DONOVAN, *Conflict and Crisis: The Presidency of Harry S. Truman, 1945–1948*. New York: Norton, 1977.

ROBERT H. FERRELL, *Harry S. Truman and the Modern American Presidency*. Boston: Little, Brown, 1983.

ALONZO L. HAMBY, *Beyond the New Deal: Harry S. Truman and American Liberalism*. New York: Columbia University Press, 1973.

ALONZO L. HAMBY, ED., *Harry S. Truman and the Fair Deal*. Lexington, MA: D.C. Heath, 1974.

MICHAEL J. HOGAN, *A Cross of Iron: Harry S. Truman and the Origins of the National Security State, 1945–1954*. Cambridge, UK: Cambridge University Press, 1998.

ROY JENKINS, *Truman*. New York: Harper and Row, 1986.

R. ALTON LEE, *Truman and Taft-Hartley: A Question of Mandate*. Lexington: University of Kentucky Press, 1966.

DONALD R. MCCOY AND RICHARD T. RUETTEN, *Quest and Re-*

sponse: Minority Rights and the Truman Administration. Lawrence: University Press of Kansas, 1973.

DAVID MCCULLOUGH, *Truman*. New York: Simon and Schuster, 1992.

WILLIAM E. PEMBERTON, *Harry S. Truman: Fair Dealer and Cold Warrior*. Boston: Twayne, 1989.

THE ATOMIC BOMB

THOMAS B. ALLEN AND NORMAN POLMAR, *Code-Name Downfall: The Secret Plan to Invade Japan and Why Truman Dropped the Bomb*. New York: Simon and Schuster, 1995.

PAUL R. BAKER, ED., *The Atomic Bomb: The Great Decision*. Hinsdale, IL: Dryden Press, 1976.

HANSON W. BALDWIN, *Great Mistakes of the War*. New York: Harper and Brothers, 1949.

ROBERT H. FERRELL, ED., *Harry S. Truman and the Bomb: A Documentary History*. Worland, WY: High Plains, 1996.

LEN GIOVANNITTI AND FRED FREED, *The Decision to Drop the Bomb*. New York: Coward-McCann, 1965.

GREGG HERKEN, *The Winning Weapon: The Atomic Bomb in the Cold War, 1945–1950*. New York: Knopf, 1980.

SAMUEL ELIOT MORISON, *History of United States Naval Operations in World War II, Volume Fourteen: Victory in the Pacific, 1945*. Boston: Little, Brown, 1961.

HENRY L. STIMSON AND MCGEORGE BUNDY, *On Active Service in Peace and War*. New York: Harper and Brothers, 1947.

RONALD TAKAKI, *Hiroshima: Why America Dropped the Atomic Bomb*. Boston: Little, Brown, 1995.

THE REBUILDING OF EUROPE AND BEGINNING OF THE COLD WAR

ALLEN W. DULLES, *The Marshall Plan*. Providence, RI: Berg, 1993.

LYNN BOYD HINDS AND THEODORE OTTO WINDT JR., *The Cold War*

as Rhetoric: The Beginnings, 1945–1950. New York: Praeger, 1991.

MELVIN P. LEFFLER, *A Preponderance of Power: National Security, the Truman Administration, and the Cold War*. Stanford, CA: Stanford University Press, 1992.

GEORGE C. MARSHALL, *George C. Marshall: Interviews and Reminiscences for Forrest C. Pogue*. Lexington, VA: G.C. Marshall Research Foundation, 1991.

RICHARD MAYNE, *The Recovery of Europe: From Devastation to Unity*. New York: Harper and Row, 1970.

MARTIN MCCAULEY, *The Origins of the Cold War: 1941–1949*. London: Longman, 1983.

CHARLES L. MEE JR., *The Marshall Plan: The Launching of the Pax Americana*. New York: Simon and Schuster, 1984.

THOMAS PARRISH, *Berlin in the Balance, 1945–1949: The Blockade, the Airlift, the First Major Battle of the Cold War*. Reading, MA: Addison-Wesley, 1998.

ROGER S. WHITCOMB, *The Cold War in Retrospect: The Formative Years*. Westport, CT: Praeger, 1998.

THEODORE A. WILSON, *The Marshall Plan, 1947–1951*. New York: Foreign Policy Association, 1977.

MACARTHUR AND THE KOREAN WAR

FRANCIS H. HELLER, ED., *The Korean War: A Twenty-Five-Year Perspective*. Lawrence: Regents Press of Kansas, 1977.

TRUMBULL HIGGINS, *Korea and the Fall of MacArthur: A Precis in Limited War*. New York: Oxford University Press, 1960.

ROBERT LECKIE, *Conflict: The History of the Korean War, 1950–53*. New York: Putnam, 1962.

WILLIAM MANCHESTER, *American Caesar: Douglas MacArthur, 1880–1964*. Boston: Little, Brown, 1978.

HARRY J. MIDDLETON, *The Compact History of the Korean War*. New York: Hawthorn Books, 1965.

GEOFFREY PERRET, *Old Soldiers Never Die: The Life of Douglas MacArthur*. New York: Random House, 1996.

MATTHEW B. RIDGWAY, *The Korean War*. Garden City, NY: Doubleday, 1967.

RICHARD H. ROVERE AND ARTHUR SCHLESINGER JR., *The MacArthur Controversy and American Foreign Policy*. New York: Farrar, Straus and Giroux, 1965.

ROBERT SMITH, *MacArthur in Korea: The Naked Emperor*. New York: Simon and Schuster, 1982.

JAMES L. STOKESBURY, *A Short History of the Korean War*. New York: W. Morrow, 1988.

COURTNEY WHITNEY, *MacArthur: His Rendezvous with History*. New York: Alfred A. Knopf, 1956.

INDEX

McKim, Eddie, 43
Mee, Charles, 126
Middleton, Harry J., 172
Miller, Richard Lawrence, 17, 29
on Truman's civil rights record,
32
minimum wage
increase in, 31
Mollison, Irvin C., 207
Munich Conference of 1938, 150
Murphy, Charles S., 139
Murphy, Robert, 136
My Fair Lady (play), 204

Nagasaki
bombing of, 20, 51, 53–54, 62,
75
National Association for the
Advancement of Colored People
(NAACP), 207, 220
National Manpower Mobilization
Policy, 212
National Planning Association,
127
New Deal, 31, 207
internationalization of, 129
New Frontier, 201
New Republic (magazine), 202
Newsweek (magazine), 57, 101
New Yorker (magazine), 204
Nixon, Richard M., 34, 177, 197
North Atlantic Treaty
Organization (NATO), 26,
119–20

Okinawa, Battle of, 19, 42–43
as model for casualties from
invasion of Japan, 68
Oppenheimer, J. Robert, 20
and opposition to atomic bomb
use, 82

Pace, Frank, 170, 175
Palestine
partition of, 29

Pelz, Stephen, 151
Pendergast, Thomas J., 16, 17, 201
Pepper, Claude, 194
Peters, Charles, 199
*Politics of War and the United
States Foreign Policy 1943–1945,
The* (Gabriel Kolko), 56
Polmar, Norman, 65
Potsdam Conference, 46, 66, 79
Potsdam Proclamation, 71
President's Committee on Civil
Rights, 32–33, 206, 220
Price, Harry Bayard, 114
public opinion
on civil rights, 208
on foreign aid, 130
on Japanese terms of surrender,
63
on Truman, 125
effects of Truman Doctrine,
101
and MacArthur's dismissal,
178–79
before 1948 convention, 136
Pygmalion (play), 204

race
Truman's views on, 202
railroad strike, 35
Randolph, A. Philip, 223
Rawls, John, 85
Red Scare, 34, 152–54
see also communism
Reed, James A., 16
*Refighting the Last War: Command
and Crisis in Korea 1950–1953*
(James), 150
Republican Party
and McCarthyism, 153
Ridgway, Matthew B., 28
replacement of MacArthur by,
161, 170
Roosevelt, Franklin D., 18, 31, 38,
201, 216
death of, 19